1,227
QUITE
INTERESTING
FACTS

TO BLOW YOUR SOCKS OFF

by John Lloyd & John Mitchinson

THE BOOK OF GENERAL IGNORANCE

THE BOOK OF ANIMAL IGNORANCE

IF IGNORANCE IS BLISS, WHY AREN'T THERE MORE
HAPPY PEOPLE?: SMART QUOTES FOR DUMB TIMES

THE BOOK OF THE DEAD

THE SECOND BOOK OF GENERAL IGNORANCE

also by John Lloyd (with Douglas Adams)

THE MEANING OF LIFF

THE DEEPER MEANING OF LIFF

1,227
QUITE
INTERESTING
FACTS

TO BLOW YOUR SOCKS OFF

Compiled by
John Lloyd, John Mitchinson,
and James Harkin

with the QI Elves
Anne Miller, Andy Murray, and Alex Bell

W. W. Norton & Company
New York • London

First published in Great Britain in 2012 by Faber and Faber Ltd under
the title *1,227 QI Facts to Blow Your Socks Off*

For information about permission to reproduce selections from this
book, write to Permissions, W. W. Norton & Company, Inc.,
500 Fifth Avenue, New York, NY 10110

For information about special discounts for bulk purchases, please
contact W. W. Norton Special Sales
at specialsales@wwnorton.com or 800-233-4830

Manufacturing by R R Donnelley-Westford

Library of Congress Cataloging-in-Publication Data

Lloyd, John, 1951–
1,227 quite interesting facts to blow your socks off / compiled by John
Lloyd, John Mitchinson, and James Harkin ; with the QI Elves Anne
Miller, Andy Murray, and Alex Bell. — First American edition.
pages cm
Includes bibliographical references and index.
First published in Great Britain in 2012 by Faber and Faber Ltd under
the title: 1,227 QI facts to blow your socks off.
ISBN 978-0-393-24103-7 (hardcover)
1. Curiosities and wonders. 2. History—Miscellanea. 3. Science—
Miscellanea. I. Mitchinson, John, 1963– II. Harkin, James, 1971–
III. 1,227 QI facts to blow your socks off IV. Title. V. Title: One
thousand two hundred and twenty seven quite interesting facts to blow
your socks off.
AG243.L56 2013
031.02—dc23

2013026926

W. W. Norton & Company, Inc.
500 Fifth Avenue, New York, N.Y. 10110
www.wwnorton.com

W. W. Norton & Company Ltd.
Castle House, 75/76 Wells Street, London W1T 3QT

3 4 5 6 7 8 9 0

Contents

Introduction

*I am no poet but, if you think for yourselves
as I proceed, the facts will form
a poem in your mind.*

MICHAEL FARADAY (1791–1867)

The son of a village blacksmith from the backwoods of Cumbria in northwest England, Michael Faraday was one of the greatest scientists in history and the greatest experimentalist of them all. He left school at 14 with only the most rudimentary education, and taught himself everything he knew by reading the books that passed through his hands during his seven-year apprenticeship to a London bookbinder.

From these humble beginnings he rose to become the greatest scientist of his day, the man to whom we owe the electric motor and our daily use of electricity itself. A century later, Albert Einstein kept a picture of him on his study wall, alongside Isaac Newton and James Clerk Maxwell.

The authors of this book work for Quite Interesting Ltd, a British company that makes *QI*, the BBC's multiple award-winning TV game show about interesting information.

Like Faraday, we read a lot of books—on any and every conceivable subject, and the more madly random the better.

None of us claim to have an ounce of Faraday's genius, but all three of us, despite the fact that we each went to college (43, 31, and 16 years ago respectively), count ourselves as essentially self-educated.

We have achieved this together over the last ten years by applying the QI Research

Method, which can be expressed in a single line. It is to "read all of anything (even the footnotes) but write down *only* what you, personally, find interesting." This not only reduces, by several orders of magnitude, the essentially infinite amount of available information in the universe, but it also has the delightful side effect that we really do "learn something new every day."

For instance, until 20 minutes ago, when we started writing this introduction, none of us knew that Michael Faraday (as in so many other ways) was more than 150 years ahead of us. For he did exactly the same thing as we now do: he read every book he came across, but noted down only what he found "singular or clever."

Core QI research always begins like this, in nuggets. Each bit is then added to our database, expressed in the clearest and sparest form that we can manage.

This simple way of distilling knowledge leaves behind a rich residue of astonishment and delight, a small selection of which is before you.

Much of what we find lays bare, surprisingly often, what is *not* known, rather than what *is* known. Such information (or lack of it) can be returned to again and again without ever becoming dull. It bears thinking about, often. When Newton was asked how he had discovered the universal law of gravitation, he replied, "By thinking on it continually." Or, as another of our heroes, Ivan Petrovich Pavlov, put it: "Do not become a mere recorder of facts, but try to penetrate the mystery of their origin."

So here, in bite-sized pieces, nestling among the known and the numbered, are the mysteries of the enormous and the minuscule; of human comedy and tragedy; of heat, light, speed, life, art, and thought.

As Faraday urged his students, we also try to think for ourselves. But more uncannily than that, coaxing these 1,227 items into an order that felt comfortable and right has had the strange result that they have indeed come to form a kind of poem in the mind.

We hope you enjoy reading them as much as we have enjoyed putting them together.

And, if you solve any of the mysteries, let us know.

JOHN LLOYD, JOHN MITCHINSON,

AND JAMES HARKIN

Everyone is entitled to their own opinions,
but they are not entitled
to their own facts.

DANIEL PATRICK MOYNIHAN (1927–2003)

1,227
QUITE
INTERESTING
FACTS

TO BLOW YOUR SOCKS OFF

Asteroid
1,227
is called Geranium.

The ozone layer
smells faintly of
geraniums.

The center of the galaxy
tastes like
raspberries.

The universe
is shaped
like a vuvuzela.

Light travels
18 million times faster
than rain.

The Queen is the legal owner
of one-sixth of the
Earth's land surface.

The name of the first human being
in Norse mythology
is Ask.

Everybody expected
the Spanish Inquisition—
they were legally obliged
to give 30 days' notice.

Octopuses
have three hearts.

Kangaroos
have three vaginas.

Three of Fidel Castro's sons,
Alexis, Alexander, and Alejandro,
are named
after Alexander the Great.

The opening words of
Jerome K. Jerome's
Three Men in a Boat are:
"There were four of us."

40% of the human race
did not survive
beyond its 1st birthday.

One in ten European babies
is conceived
in an IKEA bed.

The human heart
pumps enough blood in a lifetime
to fill three supertankers.

The word "time"
is the most commonly used
noun in English.

10% of all the photographs
in the world
were taken in the last 12 months.

Between 1838 and 1960,
more than half the photos taken
were of babies.

The words written on
Twitter every day
would fill
a 10-million-page book.

In 2008, a man in Ohio
was arrested for
having sex with a picnic table.

The average person walks
the equivalent of three times
around the world
in a lifetime.

The world's population spends
500,000 hours a day
typing Internet security codes.

The first book ever printed in Oxford
had a misprint on the first page:
they got the date wrong.

For 100 years, the flag of the
tropical Turks and Caicos Islands
in the West Indies
mistakenly featured an igloo.

One-third of Russians
believe that
the Sun revolves around the Earth.

46% of American adults
believe that the world
is less than 10,000 years old.

46% of American adults
can't read well enough to understand
the label on their prescription medicine.

At least 75%
of convicted criminals
are unable to read or write.

Beyoncé Knowles
is an 8th cousin, four times removed,
of Gustav Mahler.

Shostakovich
wrote his 8th Symphony
in a henhouse.

Argentina
is the 8th-largest country
with the 8th-largest Jewish population.

January 8, 1835,
is the only day in history
that the USA had no national debt.

Italy's biggest business is the Mafia.
It turns over $178 billion a year
and accounts for 7% of GDP.

George W. Bush and Saddam Hussein
had their shoes hand-made
by the same Italian shoemaker.

The designer of Saddam's bunker
was the grandson of the woman
who built Hitler's bunker.

Churchill's secret bunker
was in Neasden.
It was so horrible
he went there only once.

In his first year at Harrow,
Winston Churchill was bottom
of the whole school.

The Irish poet Brendan Behan
became an alcoholic
at the age of eight.

Leonardo da Vinci
worked on the *Mona Lisa* for 15 years.
By the time he died in 1519,
he still didn't consider it finished.

When the *Mona Lisa* was stolen
from the Louvre in 1911,
one of the suspects was Picasso.

Most diamonds are
at least 3 billion years old.

There are enough
diamonds in existence
to give everyone on the planet
a cupful.

A burning candle creates
1.5 million tiny diamonds
per second.

Under extreme high pressure,
diamonds can be made
from peanut butter.

The US tax code
is four times as long
as the complete works of Shakespeare.

Shakespeare, Sir Walter Raleigh,
and King Charles I
all had pierced ears.

An "earworm" is a song
that gets stuck in your head.

Over 100 billion neutrinos
pass unnoticed through your head
every second.

Q

IKEA
is the world's 3rd-largest user
of wood and sells 2 billion
Swedish meatballs a year.

In Afghanistan and Iraq
it takes 250,000 bullets
(three tons of ammunition)
to kill each insurgent.

More British veterans
of the Falklands conflict
have committed suicide since the war
than were killed during it.

A language
dies every 14 days.

The world's largest pearl
weighs 14 pounds.

On average, American doctors
interrupt their patients
within 14 seconds.

There are over 14 billion light bulbs
in the world
but fewer than 14 million Jews.

People earning over $21,000 a year
are the richest 4%
on the planet.

There are eight times as many atoms
in a teaspoonful of water
as there are teaspoonfuls of water
in the Atlantic.

There are more living organisms
in a teaspoonful of soil
than there are people on Earth,
and a billion times more in a ton
than there are stars
in the Milky Way.

Charles Darwin
calculated that English soil contained
50,000 worms an acre.

In 1999, Darlington Football Club acquired
50,000 worms to irrigate their
waterlogged pitch.
They all drowned.

Three and a half Olympic swimming pools
could hold all the gold
ever mined in the world.

In 2011, Birds Eye sold
225 billion frozen peas:
enough to fill
40 Olympic swimming pools.

If all the Birds Eye waffles
sold in a year were stacked up,
they would be 474 times higher
than Mount Everest.

Edmund Hillary, the first man to climb
Everest, was a professional beekeeper.
When filling in forms,
he always gave his occupation as
"apiarist."

The 10,000 trillion ants in the world
weigh about the same as
all the human beings.

If the 5 trillion spiders
in the Netherlands took to eating
humans rather than insects,
they'd consume all 16.7 million
Dutch people in just three days.

Alfred Kinsey, author of
Sexual Behavior in the Human Male (1948),
had a collection of 5 million wasps
and could insert a toothbrush
into his penis, bristle-end first.

Biologically speaking,
"bugs" are insects that suck.

Biologists cannot agree
on definitions for the words
"species," "organism," or "life."

Behavioral biologists
do not agree on what constitutes
"behavior."

Psychologists
cannot agree on
what "personality" means.

Anthropologists cannot agree
on the meaning of the word
"culture"
or on the meaning of the word
"meaning."

Abulia n.
The inability
to make decisions.

Astasia n.
The inability
to stand up.

Aprosexia n.
The inability
to concentrate on anything.

Apodysophilia n.
A feverish desire
to rip one's clothes off.

If all the Lego bricks ever manufactured
were clipped on top of one another,
they would make a tower ten times as high
as the distance to the Moon.

Liechtenstein,
the world's 6th-smallest country,
is the world's largest exporter of
false teeth.

In the 19th and early 20th centuries,
having all your teeth removed
and replaced with false ones
was a popular
21st-birthday present.

The road signs
of the Austrian village of Fucking
are set in concrete
to deter thieves.

London,
with a population of over 8,000,000,
is not a city,
though the City of London,
with a population of about 7,000,
is.

According to the Forestry Commission,
London is
"the largest urban forest in the world."

In 1894, *The Times* of London
estimated that by 1950
the city would be nine feet deep
in horse manure.

The Roman name for Paris was
Lutetia,
which translates into English
as "Slough."

In 1811, nearly a quarter
of all the women in Britain
were named Mary.

In 1881, there were only six men
in Britain
named Derek.

Only 4 Clives, 13 Trevors, and 15 Keiths
were born in the UK
in 2011.

Naughty racehorse names
that managed to escape
the Jockey Club censor include
Hoof Hearted, Peony's Envy,
Wear The Fox Hat, and *Sofa Can Fast.*

In 2012,
the Advertising Standards Authority
ordered a Northampton-based
furniture store to stop
advertising its prices
as "Sofa King Low."

Caterpillars make no noises
other than chewing—
though *Phengaris rebeli*
strums its bottom like a guitar.

Every year,
Peruvians eat more than
60 million guinea pigs.

In Switzerland,
it is illegal to keep
just one guinea pig.

98% of British homes
have carpeted floors.
In Italy, only 2% do.

In Japan only 2% of adoptions are
of children;
98% are adult males
aged 25 to 30.

It's unsafe for travelers to rely on
"St. Christopher" anymore:
he was removed from
the calendar of saints
in 1969.

10% of US electricity
is made from
dismantled Soviet atomic bombs.

Until 1913, children in America
could legally be sent
by parcel post.

There are 5.9 calories
in the glue of a
British postage stamp.

All the batteries on Earth store
just ten minutes
of the world's electricity needs.

Ancient Greek democracy
lasted for only
185 years.

The ancient Greeks
had no word for religion.

China
is the world's largest supplier of Bibles:
one factory in Nanjing prints
a million a month.

The dialing code for Russia
is 007.

Collectively speaking, humans have spent
longer playing *World of Warcraft*
than they have existed
as a species separate from chimpanzees
(5.93 million years).

Charette n.
An intense flurry of activity
to finish something
by a deadline.

Muntin n.
The thin strip of wood or metal that
divides the panes of glass in a window.

Nikhedonia n.
The pleasurable anticipation of success
before any actual work
has been done.

Smout n.
A small, unimportant
Scottish person.

John Cleese's father's surname
was Cheese.
Cleese grew up ten miles from Cheddar
and his best friend at school
was named Barney Butter.

Digestive biscuits
have no particular digestive qualities.
In the USA it is illegal to sell them
under that name.

In 2010, the BBC spent
nearly £230,000 on tea,
but only £2,000 on biscuits.

Caffeine is made of
carbon, hydrogen, nitrogen, and oxygen:
the same as cocaine, thalidomide,
nylon, TNT, and heroin.

The same man
invented heroin and aspirin
in the same year:
Felix Hoffman, 1897.

Heroin
was originally marketed
as cough medicine.

Worldwide sales of cocaine
earn more than
Microsoft, McDonald's, and Kellogg's
combined.

More than 7,000 Americans die each year
and 1,500,000 are injured
as a result of doctors'
bad handwriting.

Fewer than 5%
of blind or visually impaired people
in the UK
can read Braille.

Attempting to swim the Channel
from France to England
has been illegal since 1993.

The water-flow of the Ganges
is a state secret in India.

In 2012, Apple Inc.
had more cash
in the bank
than the US government.

Mozart loved billiards:
he had a billiard table
right next to his piano.

If you scaled a billiard ball up to
the size of the Earth,
it would have mountains
three times higher
than anything on the planet.

In 1903, its first year of trading,
Gillette sold just
168 razor blades.

The first advertising jingles
were written down in newspapers;
readers were expected
to sing them themselves.

There are more than three times
as many PR people in America
as there are journalists.

The Nazis made it illegal
on pain of death
for apes to give
the "Heil Hitler" salute.

All but one of the ravens
at the Tower of London
died from stress during the Blitz.

British spies
stopped using semen as invisible ink
because it began to smell
if it wasn't fresh.

Because Tonto means "stupid" in Spanish,
when *The Lone Ranger* was shown in Latin
America, he was called Toro, "bull."

Florence Green,
the last veteran of the First World War,
died in February 2012. Asked what it was
like to be 110, she replied,
"Not much different to being 109."

On her 120th birthday,
Jeanne Calment (1875–1997),
the oldest person ever recorded,
said, "I only have one wrinkle and
I'm sitting on it."

The US retail industry
makes $6.8 billion a year
from gift cards that no one redeems.

In the 12th century,
the Danish army consisted of seven men.

In the 17th century,
the salary of the Governor of Barbados
was paid in sugar.

In the 18th century,
the French navy buried their dead
in the ship's hold.

In the 19th century,
tobacco was used for "rectal inflation":
blowing smoke up the anus
to resuscitate the drowned.

Cardiff
has more hours of sunlight
than Milan.

Glasgow
is a sister city with
Nuremberg, Bethlehem, and Havana.

Toasters
were banned in Havana
until 2008.

The Dyslexia Research Center
is in Reading.

The technology behind smartphones
relies on up to
250,000 separate patents.

The human brain
takes in 11 million bits of
information every second,
but is aware of only 40.

The water in a blue whale's mouth
weighs as much as its entire body.

The ancient Romans
discovered parrots could speak and
taught them to say "Hail Caesar."
When they got bored with this,
they took to eating them instead.

The United States of America
maintains a military presence in
148 of the 192 United Nations countries.

On average, every square mile
of sea on the planet
contains 46,000 pieces of rubbish.

In 1251, Henry III was given
a polar bear by the king of Norway.
He kept it in the Tower of London,
on a long chain so that it could
swim in the Thames.

The tadpoles of the South American
paradoxical frog
are larger than the frog itself.

Historical Catholic clergy include
Bishop Boil, Bishop Boom,
Bishop Broccoli, Bishop Bolognese,
Bishop Busti, Bishop Butt,
and Bishop Bishop.

*Kuku kaki kakak kakak ku kayak kuku kaki
kakek kakek ku*
is an Indonesian tongue-twister meaning
"My sister's toenails
looked like my grandfather's."

In the 2009 Formula One season,
12% of Grand Prix drivers
were named Sebastian.

People in Victorian Britain
who couldn't afford chimney sweeps
dropped live geese
down their chimneys instead.

You are three times more likely
to die in a plane crash
than you are to be eaten
by a mountain lion.

Gerbils can smell adrenaline
but tests in airports showed
they can't tell the difference
between terrorists
and people who are scared of flying.

If you drilled a tunnel
straight through the Earth and jumped in,
it would take you exactly
42 minutes and 12 seconds
to get to the other side.

A medium-size cumulus cloud
weighs about the same
as 80 elephants.

Fred Baur (1918–2002),
the designer of the Pringles can,
had his ashes buried in one.

Fred is Swedish for "peace."

Nobles present at the 18th-century
battle of Bravalla between
Sweden and Denmark included
Hothbrodd the Furious,
Thorulf the Thick, Birvil the Pale,
Roldar Toe-Joint, Vati the Doubter,
Od the Englishman, Alf the Proud, and
Frosti Bowl.

The Queen of England
is related to
Vlad the Impaler.

When customers visited
the first supermarkets in the UK,
they were afraid to pick up
goods from the shelves
in case they were told off.

Women buy 80%
of everything
that is for sale.

Between 1928 and 1948,
12 Olympic medals were awarded
for Town Planning.

On a clear, moonless night
the human eye can detect
a match being struck
50 miles away.

In the US between 1983 and 2000,
there were 568 plane crashes.
51,207 of the 53,487
people aboard
got out alive:
a survival rate of 96%.

Harry Houdini could
pick up pins with his eyelashes
and thread a needle
with his toes.

The Sami people of northern Finland use
a measure called *Poronkusema*:
the distance a reindeer can walk
before needing to urinate.

The Inca measurement of time
was based on
how long it took to boil a potato.

Potatoes were illegal in France
between 1748 and 1772.

Samuel Taylor Coleridge (1772–1834)
liked to eat fruit while
it was still attached to the tree.

Sir Herbert Beerbohm Tree,
the great Victorian actor-manager, once
hailed a taxi and got in. Absorbed in his
work, he sat silently reading in the back.
When the cabbie eventually asked,
"Where to, guv?" Sir Herbert spluttered,
"Do you really think I would give
my address to the likes of you?"

On average, most people
have fewer friends
than their friends have.
This is known as the "friendship paradox."

Blissom vb
To bleat with sexual desire.

Eye-servant n.
One who works only
when the boss is watching.

Hemipygic adj.
Having only one buttock;
half-assed.

Marmalize vb
To give someone
a thrashing.

The modern world's
first international sporting fixture
was a cricket match played in 1844
between Canada and the USA.
Canada won by 23 runs.

Baseball—the name and the game—was
invented in England in the 1750s.

Baseball legend Babe Ruth
always wore a cabbage leaf under his cap
to keep his head cool. In South Korea,
this is considered unsporting,
unless the player has a doctor's note.

"Soccer" is not an Americanism.
It's short for "Association Football"
and was popularized by
Charles Wreford-Brown, captain
of the English national team 1894–95.

James Naismith, a Canadian,
invented basketball in Massachusetts
in 1891. It was 21 years
before it occurred to anyone
to cut a hole in the bottom of the basket.

Captain John Smith
of Pocahontas fame
was the first man
to use the word
"awning."

Aerosmith has made more money
from *Guitar Hero*
than from any of their albums.

Ferrari
is the Italian equivalent of
Smith.

98% of the 7 billion billion billion
atoms in the human body
are replaced every year.

Mongolia's largest airport
is named after Genghis Khan.
He had more than 500 wives
and a vast number of children:
1 in 10 people in Central Asia today
are his direct descendants.

Anophthalmus hitleri is a blind beetle found
only in five caves in Slovenia.
Named after Hitler in 1933,
it is now endangered due to
collectors of Nazi memorabilia.

Hitler's home phone number
was listed in *Who's Who* until 1945.
It was Berlin 11 6191.

At least 99%
of all the species that ever existed
have left no trace in the fossil record.

No scientific experiment
has ever been done
(or could be done)
to prove that time exists.

If you could fold
a piece of paper 51 times,
its thickness would exceed
the distance from here to the Sun.

Charles Blondin crossed Niagara Falls
several times on a 1,000-foot tightrope:
blindfolded, in a sack, on stilts,
carrying a man on his back,
and cooking an omelet in the middle.

Michael J. Fox's
middle name is
Andrew.

Emile Heskey's
middle name is
Ivanhoe.

David Frost's
middle name is
Paradine.

Richard Gere's
middle name is
Tiffany.

1 in 50 Americans
executed for murder
had the middle name "Wayne."

1 in 50 Scots
are heroin addicts.

1 in 50 Americans
claim to have been abducted
by aliens.

1 in 50 words
in the lyrics of the winning entries of
the Eurovision Song Contest
is "love."

More people go to church
on Sunday in China
than in the whole of Europe.

The lead singer of Iron Maiden
has a day job as a
Boeing 757 pilot.

A greeting card
that can play "Happy Birthday"
has more computing power
than existed in the whole world in 1950.

You are 14% more likely to die
on your birthday
than any other day.

Oranges and lemons smell different
due to chemically identical molecules
that are mirror images of each other.
An orange is really
just a left-handed lemon.

Moon dust
smells like gunpowder.

A typical microwave oven
uses more electricity
keeping its digital clock on standby
than it does heating food.

As it grows,
sweet corn makes a squeaking noise
like two balloons
rubbing against each other.

Emissions from car exhausts
are responsible for
more deaths every year
than road accidents.

You can legally buy cannabis
in the US in the form of birdseed:
the feathers of birds that eat it
acquire a particularly
glossy sheen.

Fidel Castro
estimated that he saved
ten working days a year
by not bothering to shave.

Wild Bill Hickok's brother Lorenzo
was nicknamed
"Tame Bill Hickok."

From 1912 to 1948,
painting was an Olympic event.
In 1924, Jack Yeats,
brother of the poet W. B. Yeats,
took the silver:
Ireland's first-ever Olympic medal.

William Blake's one-man exhibition
of paintings in 1809
received only one review.
The critic described him as a lunatic.

In 1891, Claude Monet won 100,000 francs
in the French national lottery.

Pigeons can tell the difference between
impressionist paintings by Monet
and cubist works by Picasso.
They can even tell when
the Monets are hung upside down.

There are no cubes in Cubism.
Cézanne's theory was that everything
could be broken down into
cylinders, spheres, and cones.

Tour de France riders
need to eat the equivalent of
27 cheeseburgers a day.

Lightning strikes the Earth
8.6 million times a day or
about 100 times a second.

A single bolt of lightning
contains enough energy
to cook
100,000 pieces of toast.

Pepsi
was originally called
"Brad's Drink."

7-Up
was originally called
"Bib-Label Lithiated Lemon-Lime Soda."

West Side Story
was originally called
East Side Story.

Bank of America
was originally called
Bank of Italy.

Victoria Woodhull
ran for president
48 years before women got the vote.

The smallest known dinosaur
was about four inches tall
and weighed less than
a chihuahua.

Each year, drug baron Pablo Escobar
had to write off 10% of his cash holdings
because of rats nibbling away
at his huge stash of bank notes.

The first-ever edition of the *Daily Mirror*
came with a free mirror.

After two weeks of wear,
a pair of jeans will have grown
a 1,000-strong colony
of bacteria on the front,
1,500–2,500 on the back,
and 10,000 on the crotch.

If all the salt in the sea
were spread evenly over the land,
it would be 500 feet thick.

The eruption of Krakatoa in 1883
was the loudest sound in recorded history.
It was heard 3,000 miles away
in Mauritius.

Summer on Neptune lasts for 40 years,
but the temperature is minus 328°F.

Summer nights in the Faroe Islands
are so well illuminated that
between May and July
the lighthouses are turned off.

In the 1st century AD most ships
in the northern hemisphere sailed only
between May and September.

William Carstares (1649–1715)
was the last man in Britain
to be given the thumbscrew.
As torture was illegal in England,
he had to be taken to Edinburgh.

Mussolini tortured his enemies
by forcing them to swallow
massive doses of castor oil.

The second-largest lake in Bolivia
is called Lake Poopó.
It's not a freshwater lake.

The whole of Shakespeare
contains only about 20,000
different words—
less than half the vocabulary of the
average English speaker today.

The whole of Liechtenstein
can be rented for $70,000 a night,
for a minimum of two nights.
It sleeps 900.

St. Vitus
is the patron saint of oversleeping.

The International Space Station
is as roomy as a five-bedroom house
and travels at 17,500 mph.

A marshmallow traveling at sea level
would not begin to melt
from friction caused by air resistance
until it reached Mach 1.6
(1,218 mph).

When a medium in a trance
offered to answer any question,
Groucho Marx asked,
"What's the capital of North Dakota?"

The popular Los Angeles beverage
Original New York Express Iced Coffee
is made in a factory in Singapore.

Cameroon is home to the Eton tribe.
The Eton word for "thank you" is
abumgang.

Arabic words are written right to left, but
Arabic numbers left to right.
Arabic speakers reading anything
with a lot of numbers
have to read in both directions
at once.

In 2010, the Catholic Church had an
income of $97 billion.

Trombone
is French for
"paperclip."

The word "gas" was invented by
the Flemish chemist
Jan Baptist van Helmont (1579–1644).
He also invented the word *blas*
but it didn't catch on.

The word "gasoline"
doesn't come from "gas." It comes from
Cazeline—after John Cassell,
founder of the publisher Cassell & Co.,
who was the first to sell it commercially.

Peter Mark Roget (1779–1869)
invented the thesaurus
and the slide rule.

Edwin Beard Budding (1775–1846)
invented the lawnmower
and the adjustable wrench.

In 1928, the Solomon Islands pidgin
for "adjustable wrench" was
spanner he go walkabout,
and a "saw" was
this fella pull-him-he-come-push-him-he-go
brother belong ax.

The Zulu for "Jack-in-a-Box" is
udoli ohlala ebokisini ukuthi ufuna
ukusabisa abantu abaningi.

The Malay for "slate" is
sejenis batu berwarna kelabu
kebiru-biruan yang selalu digunakan
sebagai atap ruman.

Wanklank
is Dutch for
a discordant noise.

In 2010,
Ghana banned
the sale of secondhand underpants.

No one has ever seen an atom.
They're too small to be seen
by a microscope and can't be counted
or weighed individually.

Plato thought
that the smallest particles of matter
were tiny right-angled triangles.

Since at least the time of Pythagoras in
500 BC, no sensible educated person
has believed the Earth
was flat.

A snowflake that falls
on a glacier in central Greenland
can take 200,000 years
to reach the sea.

The King James Bible
has inspired the lyrics
of more pop songs
than any other book.

In 2001,
the *World Christian Encyclopedia*
counted 33,830 different
Christian denominations.

Jehovah's Witnesses do not celebrate
Easter, Christmas, or birthdays.

For 48 years
after canned food was invented,
people who wanted to eat it
had to use a hammer and chisel.
The can opener wasn't invented
until 1858.

The screwdriver was invented
a hundred years before the screw.
It was originally used
to extract nails.

"Grading" was invented
at Cambridge University in 1792
by a chemistry tutor
named William Farish.

Margaret Thatcher
was part of the team that invented
Mr. Whippy ice cream.

A single sperm contains 37.5 MB
of DNA information.
One ejaculation represents a data transfer
of 15,875 GB,
equivalent to the combined capacity
of 62 MacBook Pro laptops.

70% of all animals in the jungle
rely on figs for their survival.

In Antigua,
"fig" means banana.

Linnaeus named the banana
Musa paradisiaca because he thought it
might have been the forbidden fruit
of the Garden of Eden.

The citizens of Kuwait
celebrated the end of the first Gulf War
by firing weapons into the air.
20 Kuwaitis died as a result of bullets
falling from the sky.

The main predators of flamingos
are zookeepers.

At the outbreak of the Second World War,
zookeepers killed all the venomous
insects and snakes in London Zoo,
in case it was bombed
and they escaped.

The boa constrictor
is the only living animal
whose common name is
exactly the same
as its scientific name.

In the 318 years between 1539 and 1857,
there were only 317 divorces
in England.

At the 1900 Paris Olympics,
events included Live Pigeon Shooting
and Long Jump for Horses.

Under the Wildlife and Countryside Act,
it is explicitly illegal in Britain
to use a machine gun
to kill a hedgehog.

In ancient Greek
the word "idiot" meant
anyone who wasn't a politician.

The Icelandic phone book
is ordered by
first name.

The human eye
can detect 10 million
different shades of color.

Wombats
have cubic feces.

Harvard University
has the largest ant collection
in the world.

It takes a photon 40,000
years to get from the center of the Sun
to its surface, but only 8.3 minutes
to get from there to the Earth.

For water to flow 110 yards
through the ground down a 1° slope takes
5 days through gravel,
13.7 years through sand, and
137,000 years through clay.

In 1969,
Apollo 11 returned from the Moon
in half the time it took to get from
Boston to New York by stagecoach
in 1769.

New York City drifts about one inch away
from Europe every year.

Between 1960 and 1977, the secret number
authorizing US presidents
to launch nuclear missiles was
00000000.

Jimmy Carter once
sent a jacket to the dry-cleaner's
with the nuclear detonation codes
still in the pocket.

Worried about his grades at law school,
Richard Nixon broke into the Dean's
office—only to discover that he was
top of his class.

The highest scoring word in Scrabble
is *oxyphenbutazone*, potentially earning
1,178 points.
(It's a drug used to treat arthritis.)

A coal-fired power station
puts 100 times more radiation into the air
than a nuclear power plant
producing the same amount of energy.

Treasure Island in Lake Mindemoya
on Manitoulin Island in Lake Huron
is the largest island in a lake on an island
in a lake in the world.

The strongest creatures on Earth are
gonorrhea bacteria.
They can pull 100,000 times
their own body weight.

A dog has the same ecological footprint as
two Toyota Landcruisers;
a cat the same environmental effect as a
Volkswagen Golf;
two hamsters the same as a plasma TV.

Humans
have the same number
of hair follicles
as chimpanzees.

Gorillas and potatoes
have two more chromosomes
than people.

The average person who lives to be 75
will have spent six years
dreaming.

The word *ambisinistrous* is the
opposite of ambidextrous;
it means
"no good with either hand."

James Garfield,
20th president of the USA,
could write Greek with one hand
while writing Latin with the other.

Young Neanderthal girls
had bigger biceps
than an adult male human.

The second man to go over
Niagara Falls in a barrel,
Bobby Leach, survived the fall
but later died as a result of
slipping on a piece
of orange peel.

An orange is a berry but
a strawberry isn't.

Vatican City has
the highest crime rate in the world.
Though the resident population
is only just over 800,
more than 600 crimes
are committed there each year.

90% of the crime
in Helmand province
is committed
by the Afghan police.

50% more US soldiers committed
suicide in 2012 than were
killed in action in Afghanistan.

In 117 AD, Emperor Hadrian declared
attempted suicide by soldiers
a form of desertion
and made it a capital offense.

Jack Bauer,
the lead character in the TV series *24*,
killed 112 people
in the first five seasons of the show.

The longest hangover
in medical literature
lasted four weeks.
It belonged to a 37-year-old man
from Glasgow.

In 1715, a group of Jacobite rebels
failed to take Edinburgh Castle
because their rope ladders
were six feet too short.

The first manager
of the first McDonald's franchise
was called Ed MacLuckie.

Coca-Cola in the Maldives
is made from seawater.

A "riot" in England and Wales
must legally involve
a minimum of 12 people.
Under US federal law
it's only three people
and in Nevada
only two.

More than 1 in 20 soccer injuries
are caused by
celebrating goals on the pitch.

Slavery was not made
a statutory offense in the UK
until April 6, 2010.

Diagnosed with pleurisy,
Sir Robert Chesebrough, the inventor of
Vaseline, decided to coat himself
in his product from head to foot.
He survived and lived to be 96.

In 1915, Charlie Chaplin entered
a Charlie Chaplin lookalike contest
in San Francisco. Not only did he not win,
he failed even to make the final.

Male fruitflies rejected by females
drink significantly more alcohol than
those that have had a successful encounter.

In Inuktitut,
iminngernaveersaartunngortussaavunga
means
"I should try not to become an alcoholic."

2,520 is the smallest number
that can be exactly divided
by all the numbers
1 to 10.

2.5 million romance novels
were pulped and added to the tarmac
of the UK's M6 toll motorway
to make it more absorbent.

In 1999, more than 3,000 people
were hospitalized after
tripping over a
laundry basket.

In 1997, 39 people in the UK
found themselves in the
hospital with
tea-cosy–related
injuries.

Deipnophobia n.
The fear of
dinner party conversations.

Nomophobia n.
The fear of being
out of cellphone contact.

Metrophobia n.
Fear of poetry.

Lachanophobia n.
Fear of vegetables.

Since 1990, the number of people
living in poverty in China
has fallen from
85% to 15%.

A "knot" is something
tied in a single piece of rope or line.
Something that joins two ropes
together is a "bend."

A baby oyster
is called a "spat."

More chimpanzees, gorillas, and bonobos
are eaten by people every year
than there are in
all the zoos in the world.

In the 19th century,
sausages were marketed as
"bags of mystery."

If a vampire were to feed once a day
and turn each of his victims
into a vampire,
the entire human population of the planet
would become vampires
in just over a month.

Relative to our galaxy,
the Earth is traveling through space
at more than 500,000 mph.

The Sun takes 220 million years
to orbit the galaxy,
a journey it has made
20 times so far.

Abbey-lubber n.
A lazy monk.

Acrochordon n.
A wart that hangs down
like a string.

Apport n.
Something that appears out of thin air:
the opposite of a vanishing.

Autotelic adj.
Worth doing for its own sake.

Although Shakespeare's works run to
more than a million words,
only 14 exist in his own handwriting:
12 of them are his signatures
and the other two are "by" and "me."

George W. Bush named
The Very Hungry Caterpillar by Eric Carle
as his favorite childhood book. It was
published when he was 23 years old.

In 2012, Britain's Eurovision entrant,
Englebert Humperdinck (76), was
not only the oldest of the contestants,
he was older than more than 20
of the countries they represented.

Swans do not sing (before dying or
otherwise), although one species, the
Whistling Swan, whistles a bit.

There are ten times as many stars
in the known universe
as there are
grains of sand in the world.

The ties bought in America
for Father's Day each year
would stretch from New York to Rome.

There are thought to be 100,000
uncharted mountains under the sea.
Only 1,000 or so have ever been mapped.

Aborigines, whose culture reaches back
to the last Ice Age, have names for
(and can locate) mountains
that have been under the sea
for 8,000 years.

Just like humans,
British cows moo in accents
specific to their region.

95% of all data in the world
is still stored on paper.
Most of it is never looked at again.

The common shrew
protects itself from predators
by dying of fright.

The next person to walk on the Moon
will almost certainly be
Chinese.

Almost half of all babies in China
are born by Caesarean section.

Europeans
consume half the world's cocoa.

A single zinc mine in Namibia
uses a fifth of the country's
electricity supply.

Per gram per second, more energy
runs through a sunflower
than through the Sun itself.

It takes ten times
as much energy to heat water
as it does to heat iron.

It takes ten times
as much energy to turn water into steam
as it does to bring it to the boil.

It takes an hour
to soft-boil an ostrich egg
and an hour and a half
to hard-boil one.

It takes between 70,000 and 150,000
crocuses to make
2 pounds of saffron.

Alexander the Great
washed his hair in saffron
to keep it shiny and orange.

In 1999, a four-year-old girl
turned yellow
after drinking too much
Sunny Delight.

Russian has no word for "blue,"
only two different words for
"light blue" and "dark blue."

Andy Warhol always wore
green underpants.

25 million Bibles were printed in 2011,
compared to 208 million IKEA catalogs.

The English version of Wikipedia
has 50 times more words than
the *Encyclopædia Britannica*.

Up to 2010, Wikipedia had taken
100 million person-hours to write:
about the same amount of time
that the population of the USA
spends watching TV ad breaks
in a single weekend.

There is more information
in one edition of the *New York Times* than
the average person
in 17th-century England
would have come across in a lifetime.

Early reports of Einstein's
Theory of General Relativity,
were covered in the *New York Times*
by their golfing correspondent.

The historic news of the
first manned powered flight
by the Wright Brothers
first appeared in the magazine
Gleanings in Bee Culture.

Dune, by Frank Herbert, the world's best-
selling science fiction novel, was rejected
more than 20 times before being accepted
by a publisher of car manuals.

Ernest Hemingway bought the
shotgun that he used to kill himself
at Abercrombie & Fitch.

Leonardo da Vinci
was the first person to observe
the curvature of the human spine.
Until then everyone had assumed
that it was straight.

Rosa whitfield is a rose
named after actress June Whitfield.
As she pointed out,
"The catalogue describes it as
'superb for bedding,
best up against a wall.'"

Someone who is *cock-throppled*
has an extremely prominent
Adam's apple.

The symbols used by !$%@ing cartoonists
to indicate swearing are called *grawlixes*.

In 2011,
a pair of silk panties
that belonged to Queen Victoria
sold for almost $15,000.

Anne Boleyn,
King Henry VIII's second wife,
liked to watch him playing tennis
in his underwear.

Jeremy Bentham's body
has been dressed
in moth-resistant underwear
since 1939.

A male Emperor moth
can smell a female
from six miles away.

A *babalevante*
is someone who makes
feeble jokes.

Babeship
is another word for
infancy.

Borborygmi
are stomach rumbles.

Buggerare
is Italian for
"to cheat" or "swindle."

If you have a pizza
with radius z and thickness a,
its volume is $pi*z*z*a$.

In 1998, 10,113 American women
insured themselves against
Virgin Birth
at the millennium.

The first motorist to be fined
for speeding in the UK was
Walter Arnold in 1896.
He was doing 8 mph in a 2 mph zone.

The first London Underground
trains were nicknamed
"sewer trams."

The world's lightest metal
is 100 times lighter than styrofoam
and can rest on a dandelion puff
without damaging it.

Graphene,
the world's strongest material,
is a million times thinner than paper
but 200 times stronger than steel.

To break through a sheet
of graphene as thick as plastic wrap
would take the force of an elephant
balanced on the point of a pencil.

The pressure in the deepest ocean,
at the bottom of the Marianas Trench,
is equal to the weight of ten brown bears
balancing on a postage stamp.

All polar bears are Irish:
they're descended from brown bears
that lived in Ireland
over 10,000 years ago.

More than half the world's population
is under 25
and more than half of it
is bilingual.

Established writers and artists are
18 times more likely
to kill themselves
than the general population.

People with schizophrenia
are three times more likely to smoke
than the average person.

Zischeln
is a useful German verb meaning
"to whisper angrily."

The Italian verb *asolare*
means "to pass time in a delightful but
meaningless
way."

Hungarian has no words
for "son" or "daughter,"
but nine specific words
for different kinds of brother or sister.

In North Welsh,
the word for "now" is *rwan,*
in South Welsh it is *nawr,*
the same word spelled backward.

![magnifying glass icon with letter Q]

Gold
is officially suitable for consumption
by vegetarians, vegans, and
members of all religious groups.

The Victorians
made tiepins
out of badgers' penis bones.

Some parts of Tasmania
are so fertile that
the topsoil is 70 feet deep.

Trinity College, Cambridge,
has won more Nobel Prizes
than the whole of Italy.

The human body has 100 trillion cells,
each one a 10,000th the size of a pinhead
but containing enough DNA instructions
to fill 1,000 600-page books.

Every three seconds,
the Sun emits more neutrinos
than the number of atoms
in all the humans who have ever lived.

Neutrinos are 100,000 times
smaller than electrons,
but there are so many of them
that they may outweigh
all the visible matter in the universe.

If an atom were the size
of the Solar System,
a neutrino would be the size
of a golf ball.

The man who sees to the needs of VIPs
in the official presidential guest house
in Washington DC
is named Randy Bumgardner.

The founder of Pan American Airlines
was called
Juan Trippe.

The Archbishop of Manila
from 1974–2003
was called Cardinal Sin.

Robert Burns was never called
Rabbie or Robbie—though he did
occasionally call himself Spunkie.

The film *Jaws* was based on a novel
by Peter Benchley.
When he couldn't think of a title,
his father, Nathaniel, suggested
What's That Noshin' On Ma Leg?

As soon as tiger shark embryos
develop teeth
they attack and eat each other
in the womb.

If the three quarks in a hydrogen atom
were scaled up to the size of garden peas,
the hydrogen atom
would be 1,000 miles across.

If all the land in Finland
were distributed equally,
each Finn would have 14% more space
than Heathrow Airport's shopping area.

Human saliva
contains a painkiller called *opiorphin*
that is six times more powerful
than morphine.

The average American produces
10,000 gallons of saliva in a lifetime:
about the same amount of water as leaks
from the average American home
in a year.

The platypus and the echidna
are the only mammals
that could make their own custard:
they both lay eggs
and produce milk.

The Chupa Chups logo
was designed by
Salvador Dalí.

4,000 McDonald's hamburgers
(as many as you could get from one cow)
are eaten every minute.

Every year,
4 million cats
are eaten in Asia.

In 2011, Chinese billionaire Long Liyuan
was murdered at a business lunch
by means of poison in his
slow-boiled
cat-meat
casserole.

When eating jelly babies,
nearly eight out of ten people
bite off the heads first.

More gold is recoverable
from a ton of personal computers
than from 17 tons
of gold ore.

The gold dissolved in the world's oceans
is estimated to be worth $475 trillion:
about 30 times
the US public debt.

In 1917, John D. Rockefeller
could have paid off
the whole US public debt on his own.
Today, Bill Gates's entire fortune
would barely cover two months' interest.

Tyrannosaurus rex (65 million years ago)
is closer in time to us than to
Diplodocus (150 million years ago).

There are about 6,900 languages
in existence but more than
half the world's population
uses only 20 of them.

In English, the name of every number
shares a letter with each neighbor.
One shares an O with two, which shares a
T with three, which shares an R with four,
which shares an F with five, which shares
an I with six—and so on indefinitely.

Archimedes' number *myriakis-myriostas*
periodu myriakis-myriston
arithmon myriai myriades
is one followed by 80 quadrillion zeroes.

In 2010, YouTube was watched
700 billion times, but 99% of the views
were of only 30% of the videos.

The information transmitted
by the Hubble Telescope each week
would fill a shelf of books
two-thirds of a mile long.

In 1900, all the world's
mathematical knowledge could be
written in about 80 books;
today it would fill
more than 100,000.

In 1900
L. Frank Baum published two books:
The Wonderful Wizard of Oz and
The Art of Decorating Dry Goods Windows.

Charles Darwin's editor
thought *The Origin of Species*
was too obscure.
He suggested a book about pigeons,
as "everybody is interested in pigeons."

In the first month of its life,
a silkworm puts on
10,000 times its birth weight.

A female ferret
will die
if she doesn't have sex for a year.

A six-inch catfish has
more than
250,000 taste buds.

A full Kindle
weighs a billionth of a billionth
of a gram
more than a brand-new one.

There are more than 1,200 species
of bat in the world
and not one of them is blind.

There are 4,800 species
of frog in the world,
but only one of them goes "ribbit."

Every human being
starts out as an asshole:
it's the first part of the body
to form in the womb.

90% of baby rabbits
are eaten by predators.

51% of British women under 50
have never been married:
twice as many as in 1980.

Kanye North and Kanye South
(but not Kanye West)
are parliamentary constituencies
in Botswana.

The animal rights group PETA
claims that cows can suffer humiliation
if people laugh at them.

Wagamama
is Japanese for "selfish."

In 2009, Exxon made $19 billion profit
but received a $156 million
federal tax rebate.

Only 2% of women
describe themselves
as beautiful.

In the 1950s,
3-D films
were known as
"deepies."

Loch Ness
is deep enough
and long enough
to contain the entire
population of the world
ten times over.

Ⓘ

40% of the electricity in Pakistan
goes missing, half of it stolen:
if there's a power cut
(which is often),
they just steal the wires.

In 2011, British trains were delayed
by 16,000 hours because of people
stealing metal parts from the railways.

After Einstein died,
his brain was pickled,
sliced into 240 cubes, and
left in a box marked "Costa Cider"
for 20 years.

Sir Walter Raleigh's devoted widow
Elizabeth kept his decapitated head
with her in a velvet bag
for 29 years.

Forflitten adj.
Overwhelmed
by unreasonable
and out-of-proportion
scolding.

Forwallowed adj.
Weary with being
tossed about.

Rhinorrhea n.
The medical condition
otherwise known as
"a runny nose."

Subitize vb
To perceive the number
of objects in a group
without actually
counting them.

An *acrocomic* is someone with long hair.
According to the *Oxford English Dictionary*,
the word hasn't been used
since it was coined in 1626.
Until now, that is.

The word "unfriend"
first appeared in print in 1659.

"OMG"
was first used in a letter
from a British admiral
to Winston Churchill
in 1917.

In 2012,
a pair of twins in Kenya
were named "Obama" and "Romney."

As a reward
for winning the part of Harry Potter,
the 11-year-old Daniel Radcliffe
was allowed to stay up
and watch *Fawlty Towers*.

Durham University
offers a Harry Potter course.
It includes the topic
"Gryffindor and Slytherin:
Prejudice and Intolerance in the Classroom."

The word "school"
comes from the ancient Greek for
"free time."

In particle physics, a "barn" is an area
that covers a billionth of the cross-section
of a silk fiber. It's called a barn because
(in subatomic terms) it's so huge.

In 2010, twice as many Britons died
in accidents in their own homes
as in traffic accidents.

The names Honda and Toyota
derive from Japanese words for
different kinds of rice field.

In French, Hungarian, Spanish,
Italian, Portuguese,
Latvian, Serbian, Croatian,
Bosnian, Montenegrin, and Tagalog,
the words for "time" and "weather"
are the same.

Britain
is the windiest country
in Europe.

The Inuit use the same word,
sila, to mean both
"weather" and "consciousness."

There are five categories of hurricane.
The slowest outpaces a cheetah;
the fastest beats the world's
fastest roller-coaster
(149 mph).

There are at least 300
earthquakes a year in the UK,
but only 11 people have ever died in one.

There is no known scientific way
of predicting earthquakes.
The most reliable method is
to count the number of missing cats
in the local paper: if it trebles,
an earthquake is imminent.

The amount of water on Earth is constant,
and continually recycled over time:
some of the water you drink
will have passed through
a dinosaur.

95% of the lead
in British army bullets
comes from recycled materials.

A *squishop*
is a squire
who is also a bishop.

Muammar
is Arabic for "long-lived."

A newborn giant panda weighs
less than a cup of tea.

The CIA reads
up to 5 million tweets a day.

85% of the clicking on web ads
is done by 8% of the people.
Since 2008,
the number of clicks has halved.

The 6-trillionth, 8-trillionth,
9-trillionth, and 10-trillionth
digits of pi
are all fives.

Under Chairman Mao,
every Chinese family
was obliged to kill a sparrow a week
to stop them eating all the rice.
The project was ineffective because
sparrows don't eat rice.

Barley
has twice as many genes
as people.

Shanghai
has twice as many skyscrapers
as New York.

Scotland
has twice as many giant pandas
as Conservative MPs.

Sending a man to the Moon
and finding Osama Bin Laden
cost the US government
about the same amount of time and money:
ten years and $100 billion.

IMAX projectors weigh as much as hippos.
Their bulbs cost $6,000 each
and are bright enough to be seen
from the International Space Station.

The International Space Station
has cost more than 30 times
its own weight in gold.

In 2005,
Americans spent 6 billion hours
filling in tax forms,
at an estimated cost of $265 billion.

Between 1948 and 1998,
20,362 Israelis were killed in wars
and 20,852 were killed on the roads.

The American TV sex therapist
Dr. Ruth Westheimer
trained as an Israeli sniper.

Snipur
is Icelandic for "clitoris."

Taking cocaine
increases the chance
of having a heart attack
within the hour
by 2,400%.

Oystercatchers
don't catch oysters.

Cows carry cowpox
but chickens
don't carry chickenpox.

Cocks don't have cocks.
In 97% of bird species,
the males don't have penises.

The rooster on the Corn Flakes box
is called Cornelius.
They chose a rooster
because the word *ceiliog*,
Welsh for cockerel,
sounds a bit like Kellogg.

Welsh
has no single words for
"yes" or "no."

Russian
has no word for
"bigot."

French
has no word for
"shallow."

Latin
has no word for
"interesting."

Uranium
is 40 times more common
than silver
and 500 times more common
than gold.

In Spanish,
the word *esposas*
means both
"wives" and "handcuffs."

Boghandler
is Danish for
"bookseller."

Serbia
is the world's leading exporter
of raspberries.

In 1956,
there were only 12 cars
on Ibiza.

About half a million mice
live in the London Underground.

The Companies Act (2006)
is the longest act in history;
it is so complex that
most British companies
unwittingly break the law
six times a day.

Per head of population,
Britain has 13 times
as many accountants
as Germany.

The average pencil can write
45,000 words,
or a single line 35 miles long.

Venus rotates so slowly on its axis
that its day is longer than its year.

Until the 1960s,
the only reliable pregnancy test
was to inject a woman's urine
into a female African clawed frog.
If the woman was pregnant,
the frog would ovulate within 12 hours.

Chemotherapy
is a by-product of the mustard gas
used in the First World War.

The year after
the American Civil War ended,
a fifth of Mississippi's state budget
was spent on artificial limbs
for wounded soldiers.

More than 90%
of all the blackcurrants
grown in Britain
go into Ribena, a fruit drink.

Nutmeg is illegal in Saudi Arabia
because it is hallucinogenic
if consumed in large quantities.

Mushrooms
are more closely related to humans
than to plants.

The first holiday
organized by Thomas Cook
was a temperance outing
in the East Midlands.

Beijing, Seoul, and Tokyo
all mean "capital"
in their respective languages.

Athens is the only capital city in Europe
where the air is more polluted
outside than inside.

Skoda
is Czech for
"shame," "damage," or "pity."

At least 109 journeys
between adjacent London Tube stations
are quicker to walk.

QI is the most commonly played word
in Tournament Scrabble.
It's pronounced "chee" and means
"life force" or "energy" in Mandarin.

There are at least 27 million slaves
in the world today,
more than were ever seized from Africa
in the 400 years of the slave trade.

Slaves in America in 1850
cost the equivalent of $40,000.
The going rate today is $90.

More than 80% of the world's population
takes caffeine,
in tea, coffee, or cola,
every day.

There is one and a half times
more caffeine in milk chocolate
than in Coca-Cola.

A lethal dose of chocolate
for a human being is about 22 lbs.,
or 40 Hershey bars.
A single M&M is enough
to kill a small songbird.

As a baby, Oliver Cromwell
was abducted by
his grandfather's pet monkey.

To keep someone to prison in the UK
costs £45,000 a year:
one and a half times as much
as it would take to send them to Eton.

Fictional Old Etonians include
James Bond, Captain Hook,
Bertie Wooster, Tarzan's father,
and Mr. Darcy from *Bridget Jones's Diary*.

St. Brigid of Ireland,
the 6th-century abbess of Kildare,
was noted for the miracle of
transforming her used bathwater
into beer for visiting clerics.

It costs more to make the cardboard box
that Shredded Wheat comes in
than it does to make
the Shredded Wheat itself.

The word botulism
comes from the Latin *botulus*,
meaning "a stomach full of delicacies."
Half a pound of botulinum toxin is
enough to kill
the entire human population of the world.

Botox is made from botulinum toxin.
Almost all the botox in the world
is made in a single factory
in Ireland.

The average British woman
spends £100,000 on make-up
in a lifetime.

All blue-eyed people are mutants.
The first ones appeared
as recently as 5,000 years ago.

The scaly anteater, the banded anteater,
and the spiny anteater are not anteaters
even though they all eat ants
and are called anteaters.

In the 1950s, to allow babies of students
at Trinity Hall, Cambridge,
to enter the premises,
they were re-defined as cats.

William E. Boeing, founder of
United Airlines,
had a pet Pekingese called
General Motors.

General Electric is the only company
remaining from the original Dow Jones
index of 1896. Since then it has had
fewer than half as many CEOs (4)
as the Vatican has had popes (11).

A *basterly gullion*
is "a bastard's bastard."

Batology
is the study of blackberries.

Botony
means
"having three knobs."

Seven Viagra tablets
are sold every second.

The mute swan
is not mute.

Engastration
is the stuffing of one bird
with another.

Cows eat only grass
but have 25,000 taste buds:
two and a half times as many
as humans.

In American Samoa,
it is illegal to beg
with the aid of
a public address system.

A new owl species
is discovered approximately
every ten years.

An adult produces enough hydrogen
in their urine each year
to drive a car
1,677 miles.

In 2012, the population of Facebook
passed 1 billion.
If it were a country,
it would be the 3rd-largest
in the world.

Before the Renaissance,
three-quarters of all the books
in the world were in
Chinese.

About 200,000 academic journals
are published in English each year.
The average number
of readers per article
is five.

The average numbers of readers
of any given published scientific paper
is said to be 0.6.

There are two Cs
in the word Icelandic,
but there is no letter C
in the Icelandic language.

Katujjiqatigiittiarnirlu
is Inuktitut for
"simplicity."

A barnacle's penis
can be up to 20 times
the length of its body.

27,000 trees
are felled each day
for toilet paper.

The average lavatory seat
is much cleaner
than the average toothbrush.
Your teeth are home to 10,000 million
bacteria per square inch.

The pleasant smell of earth after rain
is caused by bacteria in the soil
and is called *petrichor*—
from Greek *petros*, "stone," and *ichor*,
"the fluid that flows
through the veins of the gods."

The muscles that close a crocodile's jaws
exert a force equivalent to
a truck falling off a cliff,
but the muscles that open them
are so weak that
they can be kept shut by a rubber band.

The Royal Mail spends £1 million a year
on a billion red rubber bands.
British postmen use
2 million of them every day.

A hammerhead shark
can be rendered completely immobile
for 15 minutes by turning it over
and tickling its tummy.

Tümmler
is German for
a bottle-nosed dolphin.

99% of Austrians are German,
though most Austrians
insist that they aren't.

Austrians like to claim
that Hitler was really a German,
whereas Mozart was an Austrian,
when the reverse is true.

Beethoven
was of Belgian extraction.

There are no moles
in Ireland.

If all the asteroids
in the Solar System
were lumped together,
they'd be smaller than the Moon.

There are six vehicles
and 50 tons of litter
on the Moon
left behind by the Apollo missions.

Because there is no weather
on the Moon,
the footprints of the 12 men
who walked on it
are still there.

Most astronauts
become two inches taller
in space.

Google earns
$20 billion a year from advertising,
more than the primetime revenues of
CBS, NBC, ABC, and FOX combined.

69% of people
in the rear of an airplane
survive crashes,
compared to 49%
at the front.

20% of people in the UK
believe they have a food allergy,
but only 2% actually do.

The American secret service
tried to spike Hitler's carrots
with female hormones
to change him into a woman.

Almost 2,000 carrot seeds
will fit into
a teaspoon.

An estimated 18 million spoons,
together weighing as much
as four blue whales,
go missing in Melbourne
every year.

Melbourne
used to be called
Batmania.

Alice,
the 3rd-largest town
in Australia's Northern Territory,
used to be called
Stuart.

40% of all bottled water
sold in the world
is bottled tap water.

The Antarctic is a continent
entirely surrounded by oceans;
the Arctic is an ocean
almost entirely surrounded by continents.

The average American
absorbs 34 **GB** of information a day,
though half of it is obtained
from playing
video games.

Half the Saxon aristocracy
were killed
at the battle of Hastings
in 1066.

More than twice as many people
are killed by vending machines
as by sharks.

Placebos are 30% more effective
as an antidote for depression
than drugs.

If a tree were planted
for each Coca-Cola sold,
we could reforest the Earth
in three years.

The inventor of "Best before" dates—
originally for milk—
was Al Capone's brother Ralph.

After his wife's death,
a heartbroken Benjamin Disraeli
found that she'd kept all the hair
from the haircuts she'd given him
in 33 years of marriage.

Elizabeth Taylor
lived to be 79
but she never learned
to boil an egg.

Boring, Oregon
has become a "sister community"
with Dull, Scotland.

More than 50% of koalas
have chlamydia.

Ants can survive
in a microwave:
they are small enough
to dodge the rays.

Anthophobia
is the fear of flowers.

The Greek national anthem
has 158 verses,
but only two of them
are ever sung.

The national anthem of Spain
has no words.

Prince Charles
is the longest-serving
heir to the throne in British history.
He has held the position
for 60 years.

Some parts of Antarctica
have had no rain or snow
for 2 million years.

Bubblewrap
was first produced in a
New Jersey garage in 1957.
Its inventors were trying to make
easy-wipe textured wallpaper.

There is no such thing
as a vegetarian snake.
Snakes eat nothing
except other animals.

For 249 years,
the tallest building in the world
was Lincoln Cathedral.

Angel Falls, Venezuela,
is 17 times higher
than Niagara.

A typical bird's feathers
weigh more than
twice as much
as its bones.

Only 35%
of the average person's
Twitter followers are
actual people.

"Day dapple" is an old Irish term
for the time of day when
a person can no longer
be distinguished
from a bush.

The ancient Greek for ostrich
is *strouthokamelos*,
or "sparrow-camel."

"Influenza"
is Italian for "influence":
heavenly bodies
were once thought
to affect our own.

The Republic of San Marino has eight times
as many doctors per person
as any other country in the world.

Humans
have been hunter-gatherers
for 99% of their history.

Ostriches
can be trained
to herd sheep.

The French for "badger"
is *blaireau,*
which also means
"shaving brush."

WTF
is the acronym of the
World Taekwondo Federation.

In 2011,
the Internet reached
13.7 billion pages:
one for every year
since the Big Bang.

The entire Internet
weighs about the same
as one large
strawberry.

A male right whale
is half the size of a male blue whale
but has testes five times bigger:
each one weighs as much
as a large horse.

Ted Turner
owns 50,000 bison.

Kestrels
can locate voles from the sky
because of ultraviolet light
reflected by their urine.

Henry VIII had a Groom of the Stool
whose duty was to see that
"the house of easement be sweet and clear":
in other words,
to wipe the king's bottom.

Sitting on the lavatory for eight hours
uses the same number of calories
as one hour's jogging.

It was 33 years
after toilet paper was invented
in Green Bay, Wisconsin,
that it could finally be advertised as
"splinter free."

Sudan
has more pyramids
than Egypt.

Steve Jobs was half Syrian.
His annual salary
as CEO of Apple
was $1.

"Forty"
is the only number in English
that has its letters
in alphabetical order.

43 million
£1 coins
currently in circulation
are forgeries.

Since 2012,
all new 5p and 10p coins
issued by the Royal Mint
have been magnetic.

The highest-value notes
issued by the Bank of England are
Giants (£1 million) and
Titans (£100 million).

The chemical name for titin,
the world's largest known protein,
is 189,819 letters long.

In Japan, Tintin is called Tantan
because Tintin
is pronounced "Chin-Chin"
and means "penis."

Kim Il-Sung,
founder of North Korea,
was born on the day
the *Titanic* sank.

Kim Il-Sung's grandson,
Jong-Nam, was fired as heir
after being arrested trying to
enter Japan on a false passport
to visit Disneyland.

In the last 60 years,
more than 23,000 North Koreans
have defected to South Korea.
Only two Koreans
have gone in the opposite direction.

Korea
is Finnish for
"gorgeous."

The exchange rate in Vietnam is about
20,000 dongs to the dollar.

It costs the US mint
over 11 cents
to make each 5-cent coin.

"Hey Jingo!"
is a conjuror's call
for something to appear—
the opposite of
"Hey Presto!"
which calls for it
to be gone.

Between 1917 and 1940,
the cure for patients with
syphilis
was to give them
malaria.

Gatwick,
the name of the UK's
2nd-largest airport,
means "the farm where goats are kept."

During the 2010 World Cup,
100 bar staff at the pub chain
Clover Taverns
changed their names to
Wayne Rooney.
The company has since gone bankrupt.

In 2007, Robert Stewart of Ayr
was put on the Sex Offenders Register
for having sex with a bicycle.

In 1993, Karl Watkins
of Redditch, Worcestershire,
was jailed for having sex
with pavements.

There is at least ten times
as much crime on TV
as there is in the real world.

Starbucks offers
87,000
different drink combinations.

Britons eat 97%
of the world's baked beans.

The last private resident
of 10 Downing Street
was named Mr. Chicken.

Almost half of all Americans today
are classified as "living in poverty" or
"barely scraping by."
46.4% pay no income tax.

The US has more lawyers per capita
than any country in the world
and twice as many prisoners
as lawyers.

The US has only 5%
of the world's population,
but almost 25%
of its prison population.

Since smoking was banned in 2004,
the main currency in US prisons
is canned mackerel.

Prisoners waiting to be executed on
Death Row in America
are given a physical beforehand,
to ensure they are fit enough to die.

In his last week on Earth,
Troy Davis, who was executed
in Atlanta, Georgia, in 2011,
was put on "death watch"
to stop him taking his own life.

The Death House
at the State Prison
in Huntsville, Texas,
offers wheelchair access.

An estimated 150,000 people
die in the UK every year
because only 7% of Britons
know how to give first aid.

When a Navajo baby
laughs aloud for the first time,
the family throws a party.
The person who made the baby laugh
provides the food.

The air breathed by a single person
in an 80-year lifetime weighs more
than a fully laden Boeing 747.

1968
was the only year of the 20th century
in which no member
of the British armed services
was killed on active service.

The London Underground
has made more money from
its famous map
than it ever has from running trains.

In 2010, the Italian government
had a fleet of 629,000 official cars:
ten times as many
as the US government.

Since its discovery in 1930,
Pluto has traveled
only a third of its way
around the Sun.

Walter Schirra
is the only one
of the first six Americans in space
not to have one of the Tracy brothers
in *Thunderbirds*
named after him.

Sucking a king's nipples
was a gesture of submission
in ancient Ireland.

In Vanuatu pidgin,
Prince Charles is known as
nambawan pikinini blong Missus Kwin
and a helicopter is a
mixmaster blong Jesus Christ.

In 1995,
the number of TV programs in Britain
watched by over 15 million people
was 225.
By 2004, this had fallen to six.

In Romany, the word for television
is *dínilo's dikkaméngro* or
"fool's looking-box."

In the film industry, a "mickey"
is a gentle camera move forwards.
It's short for "Mickey Rooney"
(a "little creep").

Bacteria and amoebas
are far more different
from each other
than amoebas
are from people.

Two-thirds of all the people in the world
who have ever lived to be 65
are still alive today.

There are 10,000 times
as many photographs
on Facebook
as there are in the
US Library of Congress.

Eight of the Earth's 88
naturally occurring chemical elements
were discovered
in the same mine in Sweden.

The Malay word
for water is
"air."

Kummerspeck ("grief bacon")
is German for the weight put on
from eating too much
when feeling sorry for yourself.

The Finnish word for pedant,
pilkunnussija,
translates literally as
"comma fucker."

When he died in 1891, John Davey,
a schoolmaster of Zennor, Cornwall,
was the only person in the world
that spoke Cornish.
He had kept the language alive
by talking to his cat.

The first Olympian
disqualified for banned substances
was Hans-Gunnar Liljenwall of Sweden.
In the 1968 Mexico Games,
he had two beers
to calm his nerves
before the pistol shooting.

The first recorded incidence of air rage
involved a passenger in First Class
who shat on the food trolley
after being refused another drink.

More than a third
of the world's 43,794 airports
are in the USA.

The world's largest cattle station,
Anna Creek Station in South Australia,
is larger than the state of Israel.

All ten species
of the most venomous snakes in the world
live in Australia.

Powerful acids
in snakes' stomachs
mean they will explode
if given Alka-Seltzer.

The cost of fighting
a libel action in the UK
is 140 times greater
than the European average.

After the battle of Waterloo,
the Marquis of Anglesey
had his leg amputated.
It was buried
with full military honors
in a nearby garden.

Folk healers in the Andes
diagnose patients with guinea pigs,
which apparently squeak
when close to the source of the problem.

In 2003, six monkeys were funded
by the Arts Council of England
to see how long it would take them
to type the works of Shakespeare.
After six months, they had failed
to produce a single word of English,
broken the computer,
and used the keyboard as a lavatory.

In 2001, seven Chilean poets held a reading
in the baboon enclosure of Santiago Zoo
to demonstrate that baboons
are more receptive to poetry
than the average Chilean.

By 2020, the number of men
of marriageable age in China
will outnumber the women
by 30 million.

Leo Tolstoy's wife
wrote out the drafts of
War and Peace for him,
in longhand,
six times.

Zeus had five wives.
One of them was his aunt,
another was his elder sister,
and a 3rd one he ate.

In 1672, an angry mob of Dutchmen
killed and ate their prime minister.

Half of the world's
black pepper
is produced
in Vietnam.

Feeding canaries
red peppers
turns them
orange.

The name
Canary Islands
comes from the Latin for
"Isle of Dogs."

Cat originally meant "dog."
The word comes from
the Latin *catulus*,
a small dog or puppy.

White rhinos
and black rhinos
are the same
color.

Highways
in the western USA
are based on the
migratory routes
of bison.

The Alpine salamander's pregnancy
can last for over three years.

Dragonflies
flap their wings
in a figure-eight motion.

In Bali, dragonflies are eaten with
coconut milk, ginger, garlic, shallots—
or just plain-grilled and crispy.

Salvador Dalí
was terrified of grasshoppers.
As a schoolboy, he threw such violent fits
of hysteria that his teacher forbade them
to be mentioned in class.

Kali is the Hindu goddess of
death, violence, sexuality,
and
motherly love.

The name Mali
means "hippopotamus"
in Bamanankan,
the main language
of the country.

The Nigerian navy has four warships whose names all mean "hippopotamus" but in different local languages: NNS *Erinomi* (hippo in Yoruba), NNS *Enyimiri* (hippo in Igbo), NNS *Dorina* (hippo in Hausa), and NNS *Otobo* (hippo in Idoma, Ijaw, Igbani, and Kalabari).

Over the years, the Royal Navy's fleet has included HMS *Seagull*, HMS *Keith*, HMS *Tortoise*, HMS *Wensleydale*, and HMS *Cockchafer*.

A baby cockroach is called a "nymph."

When Escoffier was head chef at the Carlton Hotel in London, he got his English clientele to eat frogs' legs by slipping them on to the menu as *Nymphs of the Dawn*.

As a young man in London in 1914,
Ho Chi Minh
worked for Escoffier
as a trainee pastry chef.

The South American revolutionary
Simón Bolívar
was, at various times, president of
Bolivia, Colombia, Ecuador, Peru,
and Venezuela.

Venezuela
is Spanish for
"Little Venice."

In 17th-century Venice,
women's high-heeled shoes
could be more than
12 inches tall.

Beckets n.
The little loops for a belt
on a pair of trousers
or a raincoat.

Callypygian adj.
Having
beautiful buttocks.

Misophonia n.
Irrational rage and terror
caused by the sound
of people eating.

Sciapodous adj.
Having feet
large enough
to be used as umbrellas.

The composer Arnold Schoenberg was
superstitious about the number 13.
As 7+6=13 he feared he would die aged 76.
And he did: on Friday, July 13,
at 13 minutes to midnight.

William Herschel, discoverer of Uranus,
lived to be 84—the same number of years
that Uranus takes to orbit the Sun.

Asked by a priest, "Do you forgive your
enemies?" the dying Spanish general
Ramón Blanco y Erenas (1833–1906)
answered, "No. I don't have any enemies.
I've had them all shot."

In 2007, a Bosnian called Amir Vehabovic
faked his own death to see
how many people would go to his funeral.
Only his mother turned up.

Baby koalas are weaned on their
mother's excrement. It is consumed
directly from their mother's bottom
in the form of "soup."

In Antigua, lizard soup in considered
an effective cure for asthma—
provided the patient
isn't told what's in it.

The world's largest known crocodile
and the world's smallest man
are from the same island
in the Philippines.

The Aztecs sacrificed
1% of their population every year,
or about 250,000 people.
They also sacrificed eagles, jaguars,
butterflies, and hummingbirds.

Hummingbirds
have 2,000 meals a day
and hibernate every night.

Seahorses
are the only fish with a neck
and the only family of animals
in which the male
gives birth.

Crocodiles have no lips
and can hold their
breath for an hour.

The Cornish for "breath"
is *anal*.

Whenever the king of Swaziland
rises from his seat,
he must be greeted
with cheers and gasps
of astonished admiration.

In 1875, the king of Fiji
brought back measles
from a state visit to Australia
and wiped out
a quarter of his own people.

Queen Elizabeth I often drank
two pints of strong beer
for breakfast.

After weekend house parties at
Sandringham, King Edward VII
insisted on weighing his guests
to make sure they had eaten well.

Lithuanian men
are 200 times more likely
to kill themselves
than Jamaican men are.

Nigeria makes
more movies every year
than the US.

Only three members of the United
Nations have failed to ratify the
UN Convention on the Rights of the Child:
South Sudan, Somalia, and the USA.

Only three places in the world
have ever changed from
driving on the right
to driving on the left:
East Timor (1975), Okinawa (1978),
and Samoa (2009).

Iceland was once called "Butterland"
because the grass was so rich
it seemed to drip butter.

After Switzerland, the world's
largest per capita gold reserves
are held by Lebanon.

There are more than 35 places
called Lebanon in the USA,
at least 38 Springfields,
and no fewer than 50 Greenvilles.

Boots fitted with springs
were forbidden by
the original Queensberry Rules
for boxing.

Victor Hugo's *Les Misérables*
has a sentence that is 823 words long,
separated by 93 commas and
51 semicolons.

When *Les Misérables* was first published
in 1862, Hugo sent a snappish telegram
to his publisher to ask how it was selling.
The whole thing read, "?"
The publisher's reply was effusive, "!"

Ernest Hemingway's mother was so
ashamed of his novel *The Sun Also Rises*
that, when it was scheduled for discussion
at her book club, she refused to go.

Within 200 yards of the flat in Islington
where George Orwell had the idea for *1984*,
there are now 32 CCTV cameras.

In 2008,
an MI6 officer was interviewed
on a BBC TV magazine program.
Halfway through,
his mustache fell off.

Hitler's press secretary didn't approve
of his mustache. "Stop worrying about it,"
said the Führer. "If it's not in fashion now,
it will be soon, because I'm wearing one."

The shortest war ever fought was between
Britain and Zanzibar on August 27, 1896.
Zanzibar surrendered after 38 minutes.

When Rameses II's mummified body
was shipped to France in 1974,
it was issued with a passport.
The mummy's occupation was given as
"King (deceased)."

Barbara Cartland wrote more than 600
books. She dictated them to her secretary
between one o'clock and half past three
in the afternoon, lying on a sofa
with a white fur rug and
a hot-water bottle.

Barbara
is Latin for
"strange woman."

Judy Garland
was 4 feet 11 inches tall: the same height
as Joan of Arc and Queen Victoria.

In the 1930s, British women working
for Directory Enquiries were required
to be at least 5 feet 3 inches tall
so they could reach the
top of the switchboard.

Charles Dickens
invented 959 named characters.
Before deciding on the name Tiny Tim,
he considered Small Sam, Little Larry,
and Puny Pete.

Dickens's shortlist
for Martin Chuzzlewit's surname
included Sweetledew, Chuzzletoe,
Sweetleback, and
Sweetlewag.

John Steinbeck
used 300 pencils
to write his novel *East of Eden*.

The word pencil
comes from a Latin word meaning
"small penis."

When trying out a new pen,
97% of people
write their own name.

90% of everything
written in English
uses just 1,000 words.

20% of all road accidents
in Sweden
involve an elk.

12% of all the Coca-Cola
in America
is drunk at breakfast.

Gongoozler n.
One who stares for a long time
at things happening on a canal.

Gossypiboma n.
A surgical sponge
accidentally left inside
a patient's body.

Jentacular adj.
Breakfasty; breakfastish;
of, or relating to, breakfast.

Meupareunia n.
Sexual activity enjoyed
by only one of the participants.

Gorillas
can be put on the pill.

The German for "contraceptive" is
Schwangerschaftsverhütungsmittel.
By the time you've finished saying it,
it's too late.

On August 20, 1949,
time appeared to stand still
for several minutes,
when hundreds of starlings roosted
on the long hand
of Big Ben.

The correct adjective
to describe a thrush is
turdoid.

If a silkworm
is exposed to pure carbon dioxide,
it crawls around aimlessly,
apparently trying to remember
what it's supposed to be doing.

Eskimos use refrigerators
to stop their food from freezing.

The Sun's core is so hot that
a piece of it the size of a pinhead
would give off enough heat
to kill a person 99 miles away.

Every living thing can be anesthetized,
even plants. Despite their successful use
since the mid-19th century,
no one really understands
how anesthetics work.

A trained typist's fingers
cover about 16 miles a day.

Every US president with a beard
has been Republican.

The Bible
is the most shoplifted book
in the USA.

The world's biggest frog
is bigger than
the world's smallest antelope.

The dik-dik is a miniature antelope
that can go for months
without water
but dies after a week
without salt.

One-third of all the salt produced in the US
is used to melt ice on roads.

British geologists have discovered
more of the world's oil
than the geologists
of all the other nations
put together.

After being annexed
by the British Empire,
the sarong-clad Burmese
referred to their new overlords as
"The Trouser People."

Toward the end of each afternoon,
Sir Philip Sassoon (1888–1939)
hauled down the Union Jack
that flew over his house
in case the colors
clashed with
the sunset.

Half of Napoleon's army
at the battle of Eylau—30,000 men—
were burglars.

The penalty for adultery in ancient Greece
involved hammering a radish
into the adulterer's bottom with a mallet.
Radishes were a lot longer
and pointier in those days.

An octopus can ooze through an opening
no bigger than its own eyeball.

Humans and elephants
are the only animals
with chins.

Sir Charles Isham,
a vegetarian spiritualist,
introduced garden gnomes
to England in 1847.
He hoped that they would attract
real gnomes to his garden.

Until the late 15th century,
the word "girl" just meant a child.
Boys were referred to as "knave girls"
and female children were "gay girls."

The use of the English word "gay"
to mean homosexual
is older than the use of the term
"homosexual" to mean gay.

The Serpentine in London was the first
manmade pond in the world
designed to look
as if it wasn't
manmade.

Albanian has 27 words
for different kinds of mustache
and 30 for eyebrows.

In the 9th century,
Ireland was called "Scotia" and
Scotland was known as "Albania."

Six ten-billionths of the Sun is gold.
If the 1,200,000,000,000,000 tons of it
could be extracted,
there would be enough to gild Scotland
to the depth of half a mile.

Beavers have transparent eyelids so they can see underwater with their eyes shut.

The Old Testament book of Leviticus forbids the eating of cuckoos, ferrets, camels, swans, crabs, frogs, chameleons, eels, hares, snails, lizards, moles, ravens, ospreys, vultures, lobsters, owls, storks, herons, bats, ravens, pelicans, lapwings, prawns, and eagles.

1,000 baby eagles were eaten at the Archbishop of York's enthronement feast in 1466.

Zeppo Marx, the youngest of the Marx Brothers, designed the clamping device that held the atom bombs in place before they were dropped on Hiroshima and Nagasaki.

Oprah is "Harpo" backwards.
Oprah Winfrey's real name is Orpah
(after the sister of Ruth in the Bible)
but no one could say or spell it properly
so she eventually gave up
correcting them.

The flowers of the coffee bush
smell like jasmine.

Jasmine is a member of the olive family.
Marie is a member of the Osmond family.
Her first name is Olive.

In 1987, American Airlines saved $40,000
by removing an olive
from each salad
in First Class.

In an average year in Britain,
trousers cause
twice as many accidents
as chain saws.

100,000 cellphones
are dropped down the toilet
in Britain every year,
and 50,000
get run over.

People are 1% shorter
in the evening
than they are
in the morning.

The London police
employ 39% more people
than the entire British navy.

Cranberries bounce when ripe:
another name for them is "bounceberries."
One that bounces seven times
is in perfect condition to eat.

Horripilation
is another word
for getting goosebumps.

The technical word
for a French kiss is
cataglottism.

Cockshut
is another word for twilight—
the time of day when chickens
are put to bed.

If all the time our eyes
are shut when blinking
is added together,
we spend 1.2 years
of our waking lives
in pitch darkness.

Every time a woodpecker's beak
hits a tree, its head is subject to
1,000 times the force of gravity.

The smallest trees in the world
are the dwarf willows of Greenland.
They are two inches tall.

The world's smallest test tube
has a diameter
10,000 times narrower
than a human hair.

![magnifying glass icon with letter i]

Antarctic islands include
Disappointment Island, Fabulous Island,
Desolation Island, Monumental Island,
Inexpressible Island, Pourquoi Pas Island,
Shag Island, Circumcision Island, and
Shoe Island.

In 2008, Usain Bolt
set the world record for the 100 meters
with one shoelace undone.

Every electron in the universe
knows about the state of
every other electron.

Honeybees
always know where the Sun is,
even if it's
on the other side of the world.

The national anthem of Bangladesh
includes the lines:
"The fragrance from your mango groves
Makes me wild with joy."

One in three men in Britain
of Bangladeshi origin
works as a waiter.

Towels are a central part
of the culture in Belarus,
even appearing on the country's flag.
At a traditional Belarusian wedding,
the bride walks to the church
dragging a towel.

13% of Belarus
is swamp.

In 2011, a 61-year-old woman
gave birth to her own grandson.
The baby was conceived with an egg
donated by her 35-year-old daughter.

The American Psychiatric Association
listed homosexuality
as a mental illness
until 1973.

Sudan is the only country
that still has crucifixion
as an official form
of capital punishment.

By the age of 18,
the average American child
will have seen 200,000
murders on television.

In German,
a *Turnbeutelvergesser*
is a boy who's too scrawny
for school sports and "forgets"
to bring his gym bag.

Schattenparker
is German for someone
who parks his car in the shade.

Depp
means "twit"
in German.

Thud!
the Discworld novel by Terry Pratchett,
is published in Germany as
Klonk!

The Basque word
for "cold" is
hotz.

The Russian word
for "sock" is pronounced
"no sock."

If you say the letters S.O.C.K.S.
aloud in English, you will find yourself
pronouncing the Spanish for
"it is what it is"
almost perfectly.

If you forget the tilde (~)
over an N when asking
how old someone is in Spanish,
you will end up asking them
how many anuses they have.

When Montenegro became
independent from Yugoslavia,
its Internet domain name went from being
.yu to .me.

The Irish word *leis* (pronounced "lesh")
has four different meanings.
Bhí leis leis leis leis means
"His thigh was naked also."

A *bourdaloue* was a gravy-boat–like
receptacle that ladies would squeeze
between their thighs
if they needed to urinate at court
in Georgian England.

George W. Bush, Dick Cheney, and
Donald Rumsfeld
all have slime-mold beetles
named after them.

Since 1700, new beetle species
have been discovered
at the rate of
one every six hours.

The short-circuit beetle is so named
because it eats the lead covering
of telephone cables.

Cartwrightia cartwrighti is a scarab beetle
described by Oscar L. Cartwright.
As you are not supposed to name
a species after yourself,
he claimed to have named it
after his brother.

Deathwatch beetles
attract mates
by repeatedly banging
their heads on the floor.

During his first teaching job in 1925,
Evelyn Waugh set out
to drown himself at sea,
but turned back
after being stung by a jellyfish.

The Irish name for jellyfish is
smugairle róin,
which literally translates as
"seal's snot."

The French
for a walkie-talkie is
un talkie walkie.

The Eiffel Tower
has the same nickname
that Margaret Thatcher had:
La Dame de Fer ("The Iron Lady").

Crime, disease, and average
walking speed increase by 15%
as a city doubles in size.

People all over the world
are walking 10% faster
than they did a decade ago.

Airlines all over the world are flying
10% slower than they did in 1960
(to save on fuel costs).

As an apple falls to Earth,
the Earth falls very, very slightly
toward the apple.

Isaac Newton served as MP for Cambridge
but spoke in the House only once.
He asked for a window to be closed
because it was drafty.

Bram Stoker,
the author of *Dracula*,
married Oscar Wilde's
first girlfriend.

Arthur Ransome,
author of *Swallows and Amazons*,
married Trotsky's secretary.

Two-thirds of all the poetry
sold in the UK by living poets
is by Seamus Heaney.

The Slavonic name
for God is
Bog.

In 1568, the Catholic Church
condemned the entire population of
the Netherlands to death for heresy.

In the 1930s, the Rev. Frederick Densham
of Warleggan in Cornwall
alienated his flock by painting the church
blue and red, surrounding his rectory
with barbed wire, and replacing
the congregation with
cardboard cutouts.

Stalin had shamans
thrown out of helicopters
to give them a chance to
prove that they could fly.

It is most likely to be raining
at 7 a.m.
and least likely
at 3 a.m.

In Maori,
the word Maori
means "normal."

Princess Anne
was the only woman
not to be gender-tested
at the 1976 Montreal Olympics.

Anne, Duc de Montmorency (1493–1567),
was a French general and politician.
He was named after his mother,
Anne Pot.

Pol Pot,
the Cambodian dictator
responsible for the deaths
of 21% of his country's people,
was a former
geography teacher.

The Swahili word
for a coconut is
nazi.

"Mother-in-law"
is an anagram of
"Hitler woman."

Both Stalin and Hans Christian Andersen
were the sons of a cobbler and a
washerwoman.

In 1187, as a symbol of unity
between their two countries,
Richard I of England
spent a night in the same bed
as Philip II of France.

In 1381, Richard II made Chelmsford
the capital of England
for one week.

In 1517, Richard Foxe,
the blind bishop of Winchester,
founded Corpus Christi College, Oxford.
On his first visit to the new college,
he was led twice around the main quad
to make it seem bigger than it really was.

In 1953, Keith Richards's musical career
began as a choirboy
singing at the Queen's coronation.

No male jaguar
has ever successfully mated
with a female tiger:
if it were to happen, the resulting animal
would be known as
a "jagger."

Early draft names for
Walt Disney's seven dwarfs included
Flabby, Dirty, Shifty,
Lazy, Burpy, Baldy,
and Biggo-Ego.

Strictly speaking,
the plural of dwarf
is dwarrows.

In 2011, Toyota announced that
the official plural of Prius was
Prii.

Research using rabbits
has led to 26 Nobel Prizes
for Physiology or Medicine.

To process their food
with maximum efficiency,
rabbits swallow up to
80% of their own feces.

The Sumatran rabbit
is so rare and shy
that the nearest humans
have no word for it in their language.

Bugs Bunny
is not a rabbit
but a hare.

The sloth is the only animal
named after one of the Seven Deadly Sins.
During the rainy season,
its metabolism slows down so much
that it can starve to death
on a full stomach.

Dolphins shed
the top layer of their skin
every two hours.

Paper can be recycled only six times.
After that, the fibers
are too weak to hold together.

A 2011 study by Nobel Economics laureate
Daniel Kahneman of 25 top Wall Street
traders found that they were
no more consistently successful
than a chimpanzee tossing a coin.

A 2011 study in the journal *Psychology,
Crime and Law* tested 39 British senior
managers and CEOs and found that they
had more psychopathic tendencies
than patients in Broadmoor.

Since 1980, the salaries of executives in
FTSE 100 companies have risen by 4,000%
compared to 300% for their employees.

An average pay raise of 50% in 2010
took the annual earnings of the directors
of Britain's FTSE 100 companies
to £2.7 million each: over 100 times
the national average.

At the end of 2011,
the FTSE index stood at 5572:
1358 points lower
than it was at the end of 1999.

Google
was originally called
Back-Rub.

The *acnestis*
is the part of the back
that is impossible to scratch.

The most common treatment
for angina is
nitroglycerin.
It comes in pills, sprays, or patches.

All-Bran
is only
87% bran.

Malo kingi is a jellyfish
named after Robert King,
an American tourist
who died in Australia
after being stung by one.

The man after whom
Parkinson's disease is named
was once arrested for plotting
to assassinate George III
with a poisoned dart.

The man after whom
Tourette's syndrome is named
was shot in the head
by one of his patients.

Spix's macaw
is named after
the first man to shoot one.

Brigham Young,
founder of Salt Lake City,
had 55 wives.

Until 1857, it was legal for
British husbands to sell their wives.
The going rate was £3,000
(£223,000 in today's money).

King Herod's first wife
was called Doris.

Thomas Edison
proposed to his second wife
in Morse code.

The first escalator was for fun,
rather than for practical purposes.
It was installed at Coney Island
in New York and ridden by 75,000 people
in its first two weeks.

Attendants bearing brandy and
smelling salts stood at the top of the first
escalator in Harrods, to revive shoppers
who became lightheaded on the ride.

At least one person a week in the UK
officially changes their middle name
to "Danger."

In the American Civil War,
2% of the population died.
The equivalent today
would be 6,278,280 deaths.

At the age of 19, J. S. Bach
walked 420 miles to see
a performance by the composer
Buxtehude.

To *chork*
is to make a noise like feet
walking in waterlogged shoes.

J'ai des rossignols
("I've got nightingales")
is French for
unexplained noises
coming from a car.

250,000 birds were killed
by the *Exxon Valdez* oil spill in 1989.
About the same number die
from crashing into window glass
in the US every day.

Only half the passengers and crew
who reached America on the *Mayflower*
in November 1620
survived until the following spring.

Two-thirds of the world's caviar
is eaten aboard
the *QE2*.

There are 35,112 golf courses
in the world,
half of them in the USA.

All the world's golf courses put together
cover more land area
than the Bahamas.

The land around the Iron Curtain
lay untouched for decades. In 1989,
it was turned into a nature reserve
870 miles long, but less than
220 yards wide.

Victorian guidebooks advised women
to put pins in their mouths
to avoid being kissed in the dark
when trains went through tunnels.

Beekeeping is illegal under the
New York City Health Code,
because bees are
"naturally inclined to do harm."

Herring talk out of their asses,
communicating by firing bubbles from
their backsides that sound like
high-pitched raspberries.

The filament of the first
commercial light bulb,
patented by Thomas Edison in 1880,
was made of bamboo.

The tall chef's hat, or *toque blanche*,
traditionally had a hundred pleats
to represent the number of ways
an egg could be cooked.

It was once suggested that
New York should be called Brimaquonx,
combining the names
of all the city's boroughs—
Brooklyn, Staten Island, Manhattan,
Queens, and the Bronx—
into one.

Tibet has a smaller GDP than Malta,
but is 4,000 times its size.

Hamesucken
is the crime of assaulting someone
in their own home.

Hapax legomenon
describes a word or phrase
that has been used only once.

Haptodysphoria
is the feeling you get from
running your nails
down a blackboard.

Hydrophobophobia
is the fear of
hydrophobia.

Women buy
85% of the world's Valentine cards and
96% of all the candles
in America.

Einstein
gave his $32,000 Nobel Prize money to
his first wife, Mileva,
as part of their divorce settlement.

The best-selling work of fiction
of the 15th century was
The Tale of the Two Lovers,
an erotic novel by the man who later
became Pope Pius II.

Tiramisu
means "pick me up"
in Italian.

The names of the English rivers
Amber, Avon, Axe, Esk, Exe, Ouse,
Humber, Irwell, Thames, and Tyne
all mean "river" or "water"
in various ancient languages.

There are no rivers
in Saudi Arabia.

The Onyx River
is the only river in Antarctica.
It flows for just 60 days a year
in high summer.

The river with the largest
discharge volume
in Albania is the Seman.
About 100 miles north of the Seman
is the small town of
Puke.

The gold medals at London 2012
were the largest and heaviest
ever awarded at a Summer Olympics,
but are only 1.34% gold.

In 1979, the Uruguayan soccer player
Daniel Allende transferred
from Central Español to Rentistas
for a fee of 550 beefsteaks,
to be paid in installments
of 25 steaks a week.

In 1937, Gillingham FC
sold one of their players to Aston Villa for
three secondhand turnstiles,
two goalkeepers' sweaters, three cans of
weedkiller, and an old typewriter.

Typewriters used to be known as
"literary pianos."

The raw materials needed to make a
desktop computer, including
530 lbs. of fossil fuels,
50 lbs. of chemicals, and
3,330 lbs. of water,
weigh two tons:
about the same as a rhinoceros.

Exocet is French for
"flying fish."

Ancient Scandinavians
believed that the Aurora Borealis was
the result of huge shoals of herring
reflecting light into the sky.

The word "döner"
in *döner kebab*
is Turkish for
"rotating."

Woodrow Wilson
kept a flock of sheep
on the White House lawn.
He sold the wool and gave the money
to the Red Cross.

Bill Clinton
was mauled by a sheep
at the age of eight and didn't learn
to ride a bicycle until he was 22.

Before signing the trade embargo
against Cuba, John F. Kennedy
got his press secretary to buy him
1,000 Cuban cigars.

Ronald Reagan's pet name for
Nancy Reagan was
"Mommy Poo Pants."

After George W. Bush
was re-elected president in 2004,
the number of calls from US citizens
to the Canadian Immigration authorities
jumped from 20,000 to 115,000 a day.

One of the main contributors
to the original *Oxford English Dictionary*
cut off his penis in a fit of madness.

The longest palindrome in the
Oxford English Dictionary is "tattarrattat."
James Joyce used it in *Ulysses*:
"I knew his tattarrattat at the door."

The longest palindrome written by one
poet about another is W. H. Auden's:
"T. Eliot, top bard, notes putrid tang
emanating, is sad. I'd assign it a name:
Gnat dirt upset on drab pot toilet."

Q.

James Joyce
married a woman named Nora Barnacle.
She once asked him,
"Why don't you write books
people can read?"

During rehearsals for *Peter Pan*,
J. M. Barrie ordered Brussels sprouts
every day for lunch, but never ate them.
When asked why, he said:
"I cannot resist ordering them.
The words are so lovely to say."

Botanists
cannot tell the difference
between broccoli and cauliflower.

Rhubarb
is a vegetable.

Some species of scorpion
survive on one meal
a year.

The Brazilian state of Rio Grande do Sul
has only 5% of the country's population
but provides 70% of its fashion models.

The trap-jaw ant
has the fastest bite in the world:
its jaws close 2,300 times faster
than a blink of an eye.

Winston Churchill
is the only politician
to have won
the Nobel Prize for Literature.

In Bolivia,
the Quechua word for "baby" is
guagua—
pronounced "wah wah."

A baby echidna
is called
a "puggle."

Baby puffins
are called
"pufflings."

Baby hedgehogs
are called
"hoglets."

In 19th-century Britain,
"mock-turtle" soup was often
made from cow fetuses.

Dogs can smell where electric current
has been and human fingerprints
that are a week old.

Lord Byron's mail often contained
locks of hair from adoring female fans.
Some of the clippings he sent them
in return actually came from
his pet Newfoundland dog,
Boatswain.

As soon as Lord Byron left England
for the last time in 1816, his creditors
entered his home and repossessed
everything he owned, right down to his
tame squirrel.

In 1899, Dr. Horace Emmett
announced that the secret
of eternal youth was injections
of ground-up squirrel testicles.
He died later the same year.

Squirrels
can remember the hiding places
of up to 10,000 nuts.

More than 10,000 seashells
had to be crushed to make
the purple dye to color
a single Roman toga.

The Latin verb
manicare
means
"to come in the morning."

In the novel that the film *Pinocchio*
was based on, Jiminy Cricket
was brutally murdered and
Pinocchio had his feet burned off and
was hanged by villagers.

Donald Duck's
voice started out
as an attempt to do
an impression
of a lamb.

Taurine,
the active ingredient in Red Bull,
is also present in
bile, breast milk, and spiders.

Sitting Bull
was originally called
Jumping Badger.

When Fidel Castro
seized power in Cuba,
he ordered all Monopoly sets
to be destroyed.

The human body grows fastest
during its few first weeks in the womb.
If it were to keep growing
at the same rate for 50 years,
it would be bigger than
Mount Everest.

To produce one pound of beef
requires 16,000 pounds of water.

The Turkish for "cannibal"
is *yamyam*.

On June 30, 1998, England lost to
Argentina in a World Cup penalty
shootout. On that day, and for two days
afterward, the number of heart attacks
in England increased by 25%.

The first violence of the French Revolution
took place at a luxury wallpaper factory.

In 1811, crimes punishable by death in
Britain included sheep rustling,
"strong evidence of malice" in children
aged 7–14, living with gypsies for a
month, and stealing cheese.

In 2011,
cheese was the
most stolen food
in the world.

Buzz Aldrin's
mother's maiden name
was Moon.

Fritinancy
is the buzzing of insects.

Most bees buzz in the key of A,
unless they are tired,
when they buzz in the key of E.

British moths include
the Uncertain, the Confused, the Magpie,
the Lackey, the Drinker, the Streak,
the Ruddy Highflyer, the Buff Arches,
the Figure of Eighty, the Anomalous, the
Dark Dagger, the Lettuce Shark,
the Isabelline Tiger, the Waved Tabby,
and the Mother Shipton.

The cake
for the Queen Mother's wedding
in 1923 weighed
half a ton.

The three
most searched-for individuals
in the Nobel Peace Prize
nomination database are
Mahatma Gandhi, Joseph Stalin,
and Adolf Hitler.

A *corpocracy*
is a society ruled by corporations;
a *coprocracy* is one ruled by shits.

The first cellphones
cost $3,000 each and
had a battery life of
about 20 minutes.

The world's first weather map,
published in the London *Times*
on April 1, 1875,
gave the weather for the *previous* day.

During the First World War,
explosions from the battle of the Somme
could be heard on Hampstead Heath.

Handschuhschneeballwerfer is German slang
for "coward." It means someone who
wears gloves to throw snowballs.

Two French kings were killed by tennis:
King Louis X (1289–1316) caught a
fatal chill after one game and
Charles VIII (1470–98) never recovered
from a coma after another one. He had
banged his head on the door lintel
on the way into the match.

Humans kill
at least 100 million sharks a year,
or about 11,000 an hour.

Female aphids give birth
to other live female aphids that are
already pregnant with yet more
female aphids.

A flock of snipe is known as a "wisp."

The bee hummingbird
is the world's smallest bird.
It weighs about as much
as a teabag.

John Ainsworth Horrocks (1818–46),
who introduced camels to Australia,
was also accidentally shot by one.
He died of gangrene a month later,
but had the camel executed first.

The Czech general Jan Zizka ordered
his skin to be turned into a war drum
after his death. It was beaten at times of
national emergency, such as the outbreak
of the Thirty Years' War in 1618.

George Kakoma, the composer of
Uganda's national anthem, sued his
government for lost royalties in 1962.
He won the case and was paid 2,000
Ugandan shillings, equivalent to 50p.

A "jackstraw" is a 16th-century word for a
person of no substance or worth.

A boar's ejaculation
produces 70 times as much semen
as a man's.

King George III's urine
was blue.

The most times a person
has been stung by bees
without dying is 2,443.

A "conscientious objector"
was originally one who
refused to have their children inoculated.

Skiing
was introduced to Switzerland
by Sir Arthur Conan Doyle
in 1893.

Nelson Mandela
was not removed from
the US terror watchlist
until 2008.

The polar explorers
Roald Amundsen and Ernest Shackleton
both wore Burberry clothing
on their expeditions.

Two-thirds
of the world's population
has never seen snow.

The French for cotton candy is
barbe à papa
(dad's beard).

The Hebrew for cotton candy is
searot savta
(grandma's hair).

The Afrikaans for cotton candy is
spookasem
(ghost breath).

Moer-my gesig is Afrikaans for
"a face you want to punch."

Before he became prime minister of
Australia in 1983, Bob Hawke got into
the 1955 *Guinness Book of Records*
for drinking two and a half pints of beer
in 11 seconds.

11 of the 12 men
to have walked on the Moon
were in the Boy Scouts.

In 1937, comic acrobat Joseph Späh
survived the *Hindenburg* airship disaster
by jumping out of the window.

The French for
"window-shopping"
is *faire du leche-vitrines* or
"window-licking."

France has 36,782 mayors,
five of whom are mayors of villages
that ceased to exist 92 years ago.

In 1992, the rules governing what the
French may legally christen their children
were relaxed. The following year,
the most popular name for baby boys
was "Kevin."

The French philosopher Voltaire's
explanation for why the fossils of
seashells are found on mountaintops was
that they had been left there by ancient
picnickers with a taste for seafood.

The French mathematician Descartes
had a theory that monkeys and apes
were able to talk—but kept quiet
in case they were asked to do any work.

Work
is three times more dangerous
than war.

A single human male
produces enough sperm in two weeks
to impregnate every fertile woman
on the planet.

None of the best-known
English swear words
are of Anglo-Saxon origin.

Under the provisions of the
1912 Scottish Protection of Animals Act,
the Loch Ness monster
is a protected species.

Before they were famous,
Clive James and Sylvester Stallone
had jobs cleaning out lion cages.

Eric Clapton and Jack Nicholson
grew up believing their grandmothers
were their mothers and their mothers
were their sisters.

Olivia Newton-John
was president of
the Isle of Man Basking Shark Society.

John Cleese, Michael Caine, and Marc
Bolan all bought Rolls-Royces
before they could drive.

The last words of Henry Royce,
co-founder of Rolls-Royce, were:
"I wish I'd spent more time
in the office."

When *The Office* first aired in the UK in 2001,
it had the second-lowest audience
appreciation score on the BBC
after women's bowling.

When Radio 4's *Woman's Hour*
began in 1946, it had a male host.
Early items included
"Cooking with Whale Meat" and
"I Married a Lion-tamer."

"Broadcasting" comes from farming—
it originally meant scattering
seeds across a field.

Scolding and eavesdropping
were illegal in England
until 1967.

Abortion was illegal in the UK
for only 164 years,
between 1803 and 1967.

To avoid being caught breaking the law
by a speed camera,
you would have to be traveling
at 28,000 miles per hour.

In 1999, a gang of thieves
was forced to do community service
along a road in Rotherham.
The next spring the daffodils
coming into bloom spelt out the words
"shag" and "bollocks."

A *williwaw*
is a sudden gust of wind
coming off a high plateau.

Mollynogging
is an old Lincolnshire word
for hanging out
with loose women.

Areodjarekput
is an Inuit word meaning
"to exchange wives
for a few days only."

A *special bastard*
is someone born out of wedlock
whose parents later married.

Although they didn't meet
until they were teenagers,
Prince Albert and Queen Victoria
were born in the same year
and delivered by the same midwife.

In an average lifetime,
human skin completely replaces itself
900 times.

The air in an average-sized room
weighs about 100 pounds.

The US navy
has more aircraft carriers
than all the other navies
of the world combined.

An animal the size of an elephant
could evolve to an animal the size of
a sheep in 100,000 generations,
but for an animal the size of a sheep
to evolve to the size of an elephant
would take 1.6 million generations.

After a meal,
a Burmese python's heart
grows by 40%.

Squid travel faster
when they jump through the air
than they do underwater.

Lava can flow
as fast as
a sprinting greyhound.

If melted down for scrap,
a bronze medal from the London 2012 Olympics
would be worth less than $5.

In 2008, archaeologists in Cyprus
found a 7th-century curse
inscribed on a lead tablet that said,
"May your penis hurt when you make
love." Nobody knows who made the curse,
or why.

The *Malleus Maleficarum,* a 15th-century
treatise on witchcraft, warned that
witches stole men's penises
and kept them in birds' nests.

The average person in the UK
talks about the weather
~~44~~ times a month to
18 other people.

The average Briton
suffers from 9,672 minor injuries
over the course of a 78-year lifespan.

Britain's National Health Service
is the world's 4th-largest employer
after the US Defense Department,
the Chinese Red Army,
and Walmart.

The NHS has halved superbug deaths
and saved 10,000 lives
in the last four years simply
by getting doctors and nurses
to wash their hands.

If everyone in the world
washed their hands properly,
a million lives
could be saved a year.

Mundungus n.
The stench of tobacco.

Quaquaversal adj.
Going off in all directions.

Pixilated adj.
Slightly mad or confused,
having been led astray by pixies.

Rasceta n.
The creases
on the inside of the wrist.

The first commercial chewing gum
appeared in 1871, after Thomas Adams
had failed to make car tires from
the same ingredients.

The first chewing gum made by
William Wrigley Jr. (in 1892)
was given away free
with his baking powder.

In 2012, Kraft rebranded
its international division Mondelez,
not realizing that this means
"oral sex" in Russian.

Before the Queen puts her shoes on,
a member of the royal household
wears them first
to make sure they are comfortable.

Spiders are extremely carnivorous.
10,000 spiders sealed in a room
will eventually result in
one enormously fat spider.

Americans eat 500 million pounds
of peanut butter a year,
enough to coat the floor
of the Grand Canyon.

Every month in the Netherlands,
133 billion insects are killed
colliding into cars.

Once a year, on August 22,
Prince Hans-Adam II,
the ruler of Liechtenstein,
invites the whole country
to a party at his house.

In online dating sites
you are more likely to come across
a teacher or lecturer
than someone from any other profession.

Since 1959, it has been legal
to marry a dead person in France,
providing you can prove the wedding
was already planned.

Warmduscher
is German for "wimp":
a person so pathetic
he takes only hot showers.

A survey of
a working-class area of London in 1915
found only 12 houses with baths.
Nine of them were being used
for storage.

One-third of patent applications
in America in 1905 were
related in some way to the bicycle.

Every year, a thousand letters
arrive in Jerusalem addressed to God.

In 2009, a retired policeman named
Geraint Woolford was admitted to
Abergale Hospital in north Wales
and ended up next to another retired
policeman called Geraint Woolford.
The men weren't related, had never met,
and were the only two people in the UK
called Geraint Woolford.

Geraint is the only word spoken
in England and Wales that rhymes with
"pint"—though in Scotland you might
hear "behint" (Scots for "behind").

There are two rhymes in English
for purple: *curple*, a strap passing
under a horse's tail, and *hirple*,
to walk along dragging
one leg behind the other.

The African giant pouched rat
can smell tuberculosis 50 times faster
than a laboratory scientist
can identify it.

Electrons move
along an electricity cable
about as fast as
honey flows.

80% of people
who die from anorexia
are aged at least 45.

A red blood cell
can make a complete circuit
of your body in 20 seconds.

If your stomach acid
got on to your skin
it would burn
a hole in it.

A pumping human heart
can squirt blood
a distance of
30 feet.

When we blush,
our stomach lining goes red too.

Christopher Columbus
suffered from arthritis in his wrist
as a result of a bacterial infection
caught from a parrot.

John Wayne
once won Lassie the Dog
in a game of poker.

The founder of match.com,
Gary Kremen, lost his girlfriend
to a man she met on
match.com.

It is impossible
to block Mark Zuckerberg
on Facebook.

Despite playing the Fonz
for ten years in the sitcom *Happy Days*,
Henry Winkler never learned
to ride a motorcycle.

The maize needed
to fill a single Range Rover's
gas tank with biofuel
would feed a person
for a whole year.

J. R. R. Tolkien
typed the 1,200-page manuscript of
The Lord of the Rings trilogy
with two fingers.

Quantophrenia
is an obsessive reliance
on statistics.

The first published crossword
was called a word-cross.

The hand jive was invented
at the Cat's Whiskers club in London.
The premises were so small and cramped
that there was enough room only
for people to dance with their hands.

Feeding curry to a sheep
reduces the amount of
methane in its farts
by up to 40%.

More than half the trash
collected on the summit of Ben Nevis
is banana peel.

You could listen to a radio on the Moon
but it's virtually impossible
aboard a submarine.
Radio waves travel
much more easily through space
than through water.

Areas of the Moon include
the Ocean of Storms,
the Marsh of Decay,
and the Lake of Death.

By law, buskers in Dublin
must have a repertoire of
at least 20 songs.

The opposite of plankton is *nekton*—
creatures that move through water
at will, rather than merely drifting.
Fish, dolphins, and humans are nekton.

When John Hetherington
ventured out in public
wearing the first top hat,
it was considered so shocking that
children screamed, women fainted,
and a small boy broke his arm
in the chaos.

In October 2008,
inflation in Zimbabwe
reached 231,000,000%.

The average car in Britain is parked
for 96% of the time.

Casanova
was a librarian.

India has almost 155,000 post offices:
more than any country in the world
and almost twice as many as China.

Chess, Ludo, and Chutes and Ladders
were all invented in ancient India.
Chutes and Ladders was called
Moksha Patam—"the path to liberation."

Southeast England
has a lower annual rainfall
than Jerusalem or Beirut.

50 to 100 people kill themselves
on the London Underground each year,
but official records state that
only three babies
have ever been born there,
in 1924, 2008, and 2009.

Women make
25% of the films in Iran,
compared to
4% in the US.

By 2025, there will be more
English speakers in China
than in the rest of the world put together.

A new skyscraper
is built in China every five days.
By 2016, there will be four times as many
as in the whole of the US.

The electrical energy
that powers each cell in our bodies
works out at 27 million volts per yard,
the equivalent voltage
of a bolt of lightning.

The Netherlands
exports more soy sauce
than Japan.

Tokyo
has three times as many
Michelin-starred restaurants
as Paris.

Bricklehampton
is the longest place name in the UK
with no repeated letters.

A vulture can safely swallow
enough botulinum toxin
to kill 300,000 guinea pigs.

More than seven times
as many people in the UK
visit museums and galleries every year
as attend Premier League soccer games.

Manchester United
is the most hated brand in Britain
and the 7th most hated in the world.

Angola has the world's best record
at soccer penalty shootouts.
They have never lost one.

Ants nod to each other
as they pass.

The Swiss
own more guns per head
than the Iraqis.

Saudi women
have won the right to vote,
but not the right
to drive to the polling station.

In Norway, "Odd" and "Even"
are common male first names.
You can even (oddly)
have "Odd-Even."

Richard the Lionheart's
younger brother, John,
was nicknamed "Dollheart."

A *smellsmock* is a priest
who indulges in extracurricular
activities with his flock.

Japanese sheep go
"meh."

Gymnophoria
is the sense that someone is
mentally undressing you.

A *gynotikilobomassophile*
is one who loves to
nibble women's earlobes.

The Afrikaans
for an elephant's trunk is
slurp.

Brenda
means "inside"
in Albanian.

Baghdad means
"God's gift"
in Persian.

The first man to use the word
"bored"
was Lord Byron in 1823.

The world's oldest living thing
is a patch of Mediterranean seagrass
between Spain and Cyprus.
It is estimated to be 200,000 years old.

The 225-year-old typeface
of the tea company Twinings
is the oldest continuously used
commercial logo in existence.

Every time he made a cup of coffee,
Beethoven counted out exactly 60 beans
to make sure it was always
exactly the same strength.

A female chimpanzee
in a fit of passion has the
strength of six men.

Higgs bosons,
assuming they exist at all,
exist for approximately
one zeptosecond—
a thousandth of a billionth
of a billionth of a second.

The Hundred Years' War
lasted for
116 years.

There are more pigs in China
than in the next
43 pork-producing countries combined.

Some pigs suffer from
mysophobia,
the fear of mud.

Tyrosemiophile n.
One who collects
cheese labels.

Ultracrepidarian n.
Someone who doesn't know
what they're talking about.

Zemblanity n.
Bad luck occurring
just as expected:
the opposite of serendipity.

Zinzulation n.
The sound made
by power saws.

The seven years' preparation
for the 2008 Beijing Olympics
reduced unemployment in the city to zero
and increased the average income by 89.9%.

Many of the doves
released at the opening ceremony
of the 1988 Seoul Olympics
were accidentally roasted alive
when the Olympic flame was lit.

More than 50% of Britain's medals
in the 2012 London Olympics were won
in sports where the athlete is
sitting down or kneeling.

At the 2012 London Olympics,
which lasted for 17 days, the athletes were
provided with 150,000 free condoms—
approximately 15 each.

British troops in India
during the Second World War were issued
the memorable advice:
"Defeat the Axis,
Use Prophylaxis."

In 1951, more than 200 British MPs
were voted in by over 50%
of their electorate.
In 2001, none were.

99% of all the words in the
Oxford English Dictionary
do not derive from Old English,
but 60% of the most
commonly used words do.

Francach is an Irish word
that means both "rat" and "Frenchman."

Argentine scientists have discovered
that giving hamsters Viagra
helps them recover from jet lag
up to 50% faster.

To *dringle*
is to waste time
in a lazy manner.

The UK is the fattest nation
in the European Union
and the 28th-fattest in the world.

The USA is the 9th-fattest nation
in the world. Eight of the top ten
are Pacific island nations, led by
Nauru, Micronesia, and the Cook Islands.

The 1 million inhabitants of the
Chinese city of Zhuji make 8 billion
pairs of socks a year:
35% of total worldwide
sock production.

In Italy, 13
is not an unlucky number,
but 17 is.

Kailash Singh of India stopped
washing after his wedding 38 years ago,
hoping it would help him to have a son.
To date, he has seven daughters.

Schimpf-los is a 24-hour German hotline
that allows customers to
release pent-up aggression by
swearing at telephone operators.

Chamois can
balance on a ledge
less than two inches wide.

Three-quarters of the French
take their annual holiday
in France.

At the 1900 Paris Olympics,
winners were awarded paintings
instead of medals.

To "baffle" someone
once meant to subject them
to public disgrace
by hanging their picture
upside down.

Edward Elgar (1857–1934)
is the only major composer
to have mastered
the bassoon.

The Wars of the Roses
weren't called that.
Sir Walter Scott invented the name
four centuries after the conflict.

A *walleteer*
is an indispensable word
for someone who has a wallet.

Before becoming an artist,
Magritte was a professional
wallpaper designer.

The playwright
Tennessee Williams (1911–83)
choked to death
on a bottle cap.

If the mass in a two-pound bag of sugar
could be converted into energy,
it would be enough to drive a car
nonstop for 100,000 years.

There were no recorded boxing matches
anywhere in the world
between the fall of the Roman Empire
and 1681.

Only three
of the original 60 clauses
of Magna Carta
are still in force.

The soldiers of Edward III
dressed up as swans for banquets.
The king himself came
as a pheasant.

The EU
spends over a billion Euros a year
on translation.

A third of the 250 Americans
who catch leprosy every year
get it from
armadillos.

90% of the bullets
bought by Britain's Ministry of Defence
are used for training purposes.

The number of ten-year-olds
in Britain who hold
legal shotgun licenses
is 26.

More than a third
of the world's smokers
are Chinese.

A lethal dose of caffeine
is about 50 double espressos.

Red Bull
was originally called
Red Water Buffalo.

President Obama's secret-service nickname
is "Renegade." Ronald Reagan's nickname
was "Rawhide," Bill Clinton's was "Eagle,"
and George W. Bush was known as
"Trailblazer."

MI5 used to own special kettles
that it kept specifically for
steaming open envelopes.

Sitting in a 15-minute meeting
uses more energy
than Usain Bolt expends
over three 100-meter sprints.

Almost any domestic cat
can run faster than
Usain Bolt.

Over a distance of about a mile,
a carrier pigeon
is faster than a fax machine.

Modern homing pigeons
find it more convenient to
follow highways and beltways
and turn left and right at junctions
rather than using their
in-built navigational abilities.

Brazil nuts
are the world's most radioactive
natural food.

The *Oxford English Dictionary*
takes 9,000 words to describe
the 45 different meanings
of "at."

A male rhinoceros beetle
can lift 850 times
its own body weight.

Alan Turing,
the father of computer science,
chained his mug to a radiator
to stop anyone else at work from using it.

The proud owner
of the first silicone breast implant
was a dog called Esmeralda.

There are only
two beret factories
left in France.

In 1367, King Charles V of France
explicitly banned the wearing
of shoes shaped like penises.

In 2008, pet hamsters
were banned in Vietnam.

Monty Python's *Life of Brian*
was marketed in Sweden as
"The film that's so funny,
it was banned in Norway."

The banning of the fez
in Turkey in 1925
led to riots, executions,
and a thriving fez-smuggling trade.

The Turkish
for "ski" is
kayak.

Dalek
is Croatian for
"far-away thing."

Smegma
is Latin for
"detergent."

The Afrikaans
for "astrology" is
sterrewiggelary.

Due to an administrative error
in the 11th century,
there was no Pope John XX.

Vatican City
is the only place in the world
where cash machines
offer instructions in Latin.

Since the Second World War,
only 20 babies born in the UK
have been named Adolf.

The "G-spot" was nearly called
the *Whipple Tickle*—
after Professor Beverley Whipple,
who coined the expression
that we know today.

Cow's hooves
are used to make
the foam in fire extinguishers.

The first potatoes
introduced to Britain
were used to make desserts.

In 1976,
one person in the USA
was killed by an outbreak of swine flu,
but the vaccine introduced to combat it
killed 25.

There are 1,000 times
as many bacteria
in your gut
as there are stars
in the Milky Way.

Bacteria
are about as different
from viruses as
metronomes are
from giraffes.

Most antibiotics
are made from bacteria.

Bacteria
can get viruses.

Viruses can get viruses.
A new one recently discovered
in a French cooling tower
was found to be infected
by another, smaller one.

Scallops
have up to 100 eyes.

The praying mantis
has only one ear,
which is located
between its legs.

Until the 19th century
the English word
for actors was
"hypocrites."

The Japanese
for "handbag" is
handubagu.

In 1947, the Duke of Windsor
bought the Duchess of Windsor
a black patent leather
Hermès wheelbarrow.

In 1915, the lock millionaire Cecil Chubb
bought his wife Stonehenge.
She didn't like it,
so in 1918 he gave it to the nation.

Since 1815, Belgium has paid
the Duke of Wellington's family
more than $46 million
as a reward for winning
the battle of Waterloo.

The First World War
officially ended on
October 3, 2010.

Wars kill more civilians
than soldiers: in a war,
the safest place to be
is usually in the army.

The world's worst maritime disaster
was the sinking of the *Wilhelm Gustloff*
by a Soviet submarine in 1945,
with the loss of 9,343 lives.

35 years after leaving school,
the majority of people
can still identify
90% of their classmates.

The speed of the wind
has fallen
by 60%
in the last
30 years.

Half of all the species
in the world live in
the rainforest canopy.

The human brain
is more complex
than an exploding star
or the US economy.

Every day,
plants convert
sunlight into energy
equivalent to six times
the entire power consumption of
human civilization.

For a million years,
the human population of the Earth
was less than 26,000.

The last two speakers
of the Mexican language Zoque
are both in their seventies
and refuse to speak to each other.

More than one in five Americans
believes that the world will
end in their lifetime.

Thomas Edison's last breath
is held in a vial
at the Henry Ford museum in Detroit.

99% of all the species
that have ever lived
are now extinct.

A Note on Sources

For anyone keen to verify any of the facts in the book, they can be found online by going to www.qi.com/US1227 and typing the relevant hardcover page number in the search box. There is also a wealth of additional background detail about much of the information. Please do let us know if you have a quibble or a correction and add your own discoveries via our Twitter account @ qikipedia.

Index

This is here to help you find your favorite bits.
Like the facts themselves, we've kept it as simple as we can.
The rule is: each entry has only one word.

If you can't find "polar bears" try "bears"; for "Adam's apple"
try "apple" or "Adams" and so on. Capital letters at the start
of an entry indicate a proper noun or name—
"bugs" are insects and "Bugs" is the Bunny.

About the Authors

John Lloyd CBE is the creator of QI
and the man who devised *The News Quiz*
and *To the Manor Born* for radio and
Not the Nine O'Clock News, *Spitting Image*,
and *Blackadder* for television.
His favorite page is 2.

John Mitchinson, QI's Director of Research,
has been both bookseller and publisher
and looked after authors as diverse as
Haruki Murakami, The Beatles, and
a woman who knitted with dog hair.
His favorite page is 306.

James Harkin, QI's Senior Researcher,
has a math and physics degree, a dark past
as an accountant for a chain of pubs, and is
nicknamed "Turbo" for his phenomenal work rate.
His favorite page is 38.